sk
Lake Baikal
Amur R.
Blagoveshchensk
Khabarovsk
MANCHURIA
LIA
MONGOLIA
ER
Peiping
Yenan
Yellow R.
Nanking
Shanghai
ECHWAN
Yangtze R.
gking
REA
Canton
Hong Kong
ENCH
HAINAN
LUZON
INDO-
D
Manila
CHINA
Saigon
MINDANAO
BR. N. BORNEO
LAY
TES
SARAWAK
BORNEO (NETH)
CELEBES
NETH. NEW GUINEA
gapore

DS 518.8 L3
Lattimore, Owen.
Solution in Asia

SOLUTION IN ASIA

Katherine Hill Pomeroy.
March 9. 1945.

By Owen Lattimore

The Desert Road to Turkestan

High Tartary

Manchuria, Cradle of Conflict

The Mongols of Manchuria

Inner Asian Frontiers of China

Mongol Journeys

America and Asia

The Making of Modern China
(*with Eleanor Lattimore*)

Solution in Asia

SOLUTION IN ASIA

By Owen Lattimore

An Atlantic Monthly Press Book

Little, Brown and Company · Boston

1945

FIRST EDITION

Published February 1945

ATLANTIC–LITTLE, BROWN BOOKS
ARE PUBLISHED BY
LITTLE, BROWN AND COMPANY
IN ASSOCIATION WITH
THE ATLANTIC MONTHLY PRESS

PRINTED IN THE UNITED STATES OF AMERICA

TO

ELEANOR

FOREWORD

This book took shape out of two lectures on "Japan and the Causes of War in Asia" and "Japan and the Future of America" at Omaha, Nebraska, in March 1944, constituting the Fourth Annual Baxter Memorial Lectures sponsored by the University of Omaha. Other ideas developed in the book come from a lecture on "The Cause of Freedom in Asia" given under the Mayling Soong Foundation at Wellesley College in April 1944. The lectures were given prior to the Bretton Woods conference on financial and monetary questions and the Dumbarton Oaks conference on a future world organization; the results of these two conferences have enabled me to deal much more positively with certain questions of the future. I have also been able to make allowance for the important military events in the Pacific and China during the summer and fall of 1944, and the rapidly changing political situation in China.

I wish especially to acknowledge the care and patience with which my father, David Lattimore, and my wife, to whom this book is dedicated, have read the manuscript and helped in its revision.

Owen Lattimore

Ruxton, Maryland

CONTENTS

SOLUTION IN ASIA

CHAPTER I

THE IMPORTANCE OF ASIA IN WAR AND POLITICS

In fighting this war we have come to a watershed dividing two periods of history. The landscape leading up to it is more or less familiar, and accordingly we often speak of World War II, comparing this war with World War I. The landscape on the far side is felt to be unknown and this accounts for an intense and often doubting interest in the future.

It is the importance of Asia which makes this war a watershed. Asia was for several centuries an area in which political history and the economic fate of hundreds of millions of people were determined by things that happened somewhere outside of Asia. We have now crossed over into a period in which things happening in Asia, opinions formed in Asia, and decisions made in Asia, will largely determine the course of events everywhere in the world.

Our ability to see beyond the watershed to reconnoiter the future depends largely on whether we have enough knowledge of Asia and enough confidence in our knowledge to use it as a surveyor uses his instruments. If we feel that the data of Asia are more or less comparable to the data of horse racing, we shall waste our opportunity at the end of this war by playing hunches in politics and treating our own future as one big gamble.

Americans in pre-Pearl Harbor Asia lived in a world of privilege; either colonial privilege or the special advantages conferred by treaty in China. The American businessman in Asia rarely had to get out and hustle. He held key positions and could afford to wait until the business was brought to him. In politics, the Asiatic was always the petitioner; and a life which demands no keener political perception than is needed to accept some petitions, reject others, and forward still others to higher quarters, does not strenuously develop the brains of the professional diplomat.

Even in Japan, the foreigner was lulled by a sense of superiority and advantage. The Japanese, not strong enough to challenge openly the world order in which they held a second-rate position, necessarily worked for long years in secret to prepare their "New Order in East Asia" before they tried to set it up by force. Although in the period between 1931 and Pearl Harbor the secrecy had worn diaphanously thin, the Japanese were saved by the fact that the majority of the experts had by then, through patient adherence to habitual thinking, developed a portentous technique for seeing through brick walls and no aptitude for seeing through glass.[1]

American lack of facility in Asiatic languages is a good gauge of the shallowness of American expert knowledge of Asia. Or, to put it the other way around, the premium on the knowledge of English

[1] On October 20, 1941, less than two months before Pearl Harbor, our ambassador in Tokyo set down his thoughts about the replacement of Prince Konoye, the slow-motion imperialist, by General Tojo, the hair-trigger militarist. Because the American press and radio were "almost universally interpreting the present government as a preliminary move leading to an attack on Russia or to some other positive action which will inevitably bring about hostilities between Japan and the United States," our ambassador thought it well to "set forth certain factors, some based on fact and others on valid assumption," which would "indicate that the opinion which appears to have been accepted by the American public . . . may not be an accurate appraisal. . . ." These included: –

1. "We think that a reasonable motive for the resignation . . . was Prince Konoye's belief that the conversations with the United States would make more rapid progress if our Government were dealing with a Prime Minister whose power was based on a commanding position in and on support of the Army. . . ."
2. ". . . indications of a willingness on the part of the Tojo Government to proceed with the conversations . . . would imply that it is premature to stigmatize the Tojo Government as a military dictatorship committed to the furtherance of policies which might be expected to bring about armed con-

and other European languages by Asiatics is a good index of the status of privilege which Americans enjoyed. The young American businessman did not need to learn more than the smattering of Chinese, Japanese, Malay, or pidgin English which made it easier to give orders to servants. His promotion did not depend on learning a language well enough to get inside the actual working processes of Chinese, Japanese, Javanese, or Indian business. It was taken for granted that the local, "native" businessman would prepare and ripen each deal until it was ready to be plucked by the foreigner. He would then bring it to the foreigner and discuss the final details in English.

In diplomacy, it was the rare exception to carry on a conversation in an Asiatic language. A certain number of young diplomats and army, navy, and marine officers were expected to learn an Asiatic language; but few of them used it habitually for social purposes. Even the routine work of reading and excerpting local newspapers was most commonly done by "native" clerks. It was altogether exceptional to find a newspaperman who could

---

flict with the United States." — *Ten Years in Japan*, by Joseph C. Grew. Simon & Schuster, pp. 459–460.

No comment is needed, except to point out that it would take about two months to prepare and launch such an enterprise as the attack on Pearl Harbor.

conduct an interview in an Asiatic language, or read a local newspaper, or who made it a habit to travel widely in the interior of Japan or China or India. Most missionaries were occupied in interpreting only specific aspects of the West to the East. When they interpreted the East to the West it was natural for them to stress those aspects which indicated the need of more money for missionary work. Many of the most influential books on the politics and even the history of Asia were written by men who could not read source materials in the language of the people whose affairs they authoritatively discussed.

It was a common experience to hear a lecture or read an article, by an "expert," describing China as a chaos of militarists, opium, squeeze, concubines, Communists, and malevolent encroachment on foreign interests. Perhaps a week later there would be offered a lecture or article describing the Chinese as a democratic people, guided by a devoted band of wise political leaders who were preparing, among other things, an unlimited field for American enterprise and profit. The American who can recall such an experience may well reflect on it. How far did he feel, at the time, that he had reliable criteria for judging the relative expertness of experts who contradicted each other?

At the time of the Chinese Revolution of 1911 the majority of the American experts (and of course the Europeans, too) were strongly of the opinion that a republican form of government was absolutely unsuitable for the Chinese. An emperor was the only thing the Chinese could understand. They were not interested in self-government. All they wanted was stable government, of a paternalistic kind – law, order, and reasonable taxes. The war lord Yuan Shih-kai was described as a strong man of the kind that China needed and the Chinese could understand. Sun Yat-sen was described either as an amiable but unpractical idealist, or as a mischievous visionary. Before the establishment of the Nationalist Government in 1928 the Nationalists or Kuomintang were described as an unmanageable horde, deeply tinged with Bolshevism, who would plunder foreign business and create nothing of their own. After the Kuomintang had broken with the Communists and come to terms with foreign business, the Communists were described as a bloodthirsty rabble who on the one hand were entirely incited by the Russians and on the other hand had neither roots nor place in Chinese life and could be exterminated almost overnight if the Chinese Government were given the necessary munitions and planes. This overnight extermination went on for ten years, until 1937. In that same year, when the Japanese, after years of aggression, made their "final" attack on China, the overwhelming majority of the experts was positive that the Japanese would get everything they wanted within three months.

This is a very much condensed record, but one

thing at least seems to be clear. America's "expert opinion" is so incompetent that usually when the majority of the experts agree, they are wrong. In the face of such a record, do Americans feel that when the majority of the experts on China suddenly begin to say the same thing very emphatically, it will be safe to believe them? The record of our experts on Japan, which will be considered in a later chapter, is even worse.

To make the experts the scapegoats for our own ignorance and confusion is, of course, no solution. The fact is that only a public which holds the experts to account can enforce the kind of competition in which good experts show up and bad experts are shown up. Discussion groups like to be told things, but rarely set their own brains to work to form an independent opinion. Yet it is a simple thing to compile the record of what an expert has said or written, and equally simple to compile the record of the editorial policy and judgment of a newspaper, showing the proportion of attention it gives to European and Asiatic problems, its score in correct and mistaken analyses, and the relation between its foreign and domestic policies. The records of Senators, Congressmen, and the State Department can be compiled in the same way. If experts had to address audiences which did this kind of homework, we should soon have better experts.

A skeptical and critical introduction of this kind is necessary as an attempt to clear the ground. In this book no pretense will be made that there are inner mysteries in Asia which have to be accepted on faith. The general assumption will be that Asiatic problems can be understood by anyone who can understand any other kind of problem. There will be emphasis on facts which others have not emphasized, but the facts will be easily verifiable. Opinions will be stated which differ from the opinions of others, but the reasons for the opinions will be plain, and they will be given in a form which is an appeal to reason, not to faith.

Unfortunately, we Americans have several handicaps in tackling the problems that we are going to have to tackle. One big handicap is our habit of thinking in terms of Europe. When we direct our political thought toward Africa or Asia, we are still in the habit of routing it via Europe. The Neutrality Act is a good example. Passed in 1939, it was drafted by Europe-minded men who assumed that the kind of war it would need legal restraint to keep us out of would be a European war and no other. It is a typical inconsistency that at the same time that this kind of thinking was prevalent, it was also widely assumed that the natural course of events would probably lead to a war in which Germany would attack Russia from one side and Japan from the other. In other words, Japan, on the Asiatic side, was taken as a secondary factor; Germany, on the European side, as the primary factor. It was such thinking that led to what Walter Lippmann calls the "unbelievably reckless conduct" of the Senate Committee on Foreign Relations in July 1939, two months before the outbreak of war in Europe, when it advised the State Department to abrogate the Commercial Treaty between America and Japan. This was done, and "Japan was put on notice that we were her avowed antagonists." Yet the same Senate Committee, in the same month, also made the decision "to refuse to lift the arms embargo which prevented Britain and France from buying arms here to resist Germany – the Germany which had been allied with Japan since 1936!" Lippmann's opinion is that "it would be hard to find a more perfect example of total incompetence in guiding the foreign relations of a people."[2]

This, of course, was written with the advantage of hindsight. It is fair and pertinent to recall that Lippmann himself, though an opponent of German aggrandizement, failed to appreciate that in order to stop Germany, Japan must also be stopped. At the end of 1938, when Japan simultaneously took Hankow and Canton, he soberly advised that Japan had already won the war in China.[3]

[2] *U. S. Foreign Policy*. Little, Brown and Co., p. 42.

[3] "Even though the Chinese continue to offer some active and even more passive resistance, the Japanese have won the war, and the operations from now on are likely to be not much more than the mopping up that follows any great victory. The consequences of the

When political situations are grossly misread both by an official body which has inside information and by America's most experienced commentator on international affairs, it does little good to be scornful after the mistakes have been made. Such mistakes are not usually the result of pure obstinacy or deliberate perversity. They are more likely to be explainable as the expression, by individuals, of attitudes, assumptions, and habits of thinking which are characteristic of a large part of the community. It is the thinking of the community that needs to be examined. The American people blundered through a whole decade of indecision and wrong decisions from the Japanese invasion of Manchuria in 1931 through the rise of Hitler, the Italian conquest of Abyssinia, the Marco Polo Bridge incident

---

victory are enormous. China, which has been a center of formidable resistance to the advancing Empire of Japan, will become a vassal contributing to the power of the Japanese Empire. What was once a liability of the first order has been changed by the conquest into an asset of incalculable value.

"In Eastern Asia, where live one quarter of the population of the globe, the Japanese are supreme. The Russians are helpless, the French are intimidated, the British position is shattered, and the Americans are withdrawn, though we are still entangled in the Philippines. The strategic foundations of one of the greatest empires of history have been, it would seem, securely established." – Walter Lippmann, "Today and Tomorrow," *New York Herald Tribune*, October 27, 1938.

and the renewal of war in China, the Fascist overthrow of the Spanish Government, the betrayal of Czechoslovakia, and the outbreak of war in Europe, to Pearl Harbor in 1941. At each crisis we moved or drifted in the wrong direction, never in the right direction.

After World War I, what blanketed everything else in American thought was the fact that America had entered and decided a European war. And when we turned our backs on the League of Nations and went "back to normalcy" with Harding, there can be no doubt that we – we as a people and not just we as a few, befuddled politicians – felt that we were escaping just in time from Europe and its entanglements.

Old assumptions and habits of thought were buttressed by this outcome of the war. Europe was made more than ever the focus of all thought and discussion about isolation and self-sufficiency as opposed to contact with and involvement in the affairs of the rest of the world. It was taken for granted that if any problem could be dealt with in European terms, it could be dealt with in world terms. If it could not be dealt with in European terms, it could not be dealt with at all.

We were as Europe-centered in the negotiation and implementation of policy as we were in debate and thought. Rather than challenge Japan at the Versailles Peace Conference in a way which might prevent concentration on European issues, China's complaints about Japanese encroachments were evaded and the Chinese were allowed to withdraw from the conference.

It is a good thing for Americans at the present time to recall that the rise of Japan was on the whole favored both by American government policy and by American popular opinion. National policy was influenced by the consideration that the danger of a colonial partition of China was not yet past. America wanted free competition in China, not the cutting up of Chinese territory into exclusive colonial preserves. The Open Door doctrine of 1899 was intended to further the American policy.

It was a doctrine of "me too," although it did not even mention equality of opportunity. America did not want China to be divided up, for fear that countries which established colonial possessions there would favor the sale of their own goods and the investment of their own capital, to the detriment of American enterprise. Since America, though now vigorous enough to take part in almost any economic competition, was not yet sure what American activities would become most important, it was desirable to ensure that no country should acquire interests which would later enable it to block the entry or development of American interests. However, it was recognized that certain "spheres of interest" had already been established in China by European powers. The American move was made to prevent a further development of spheres of interest, but no attempt was made to abolish those already marked out.

The Open Door was a consistent development of a policy America had long followed in China, not a new departure. America in the past had not wanted to take over territorial concessions in the Treaty Ports, just as America in 1899 did not want China partitioned. A "concession" was an area in a Treaty Port made over to a foreign government by the Chinese Government. Within this concession the foreign flag flew and the foreign government maintained its own police and courts. There were also one or two "settlements," which instead of being assigned to a single foreign government were international in character. American citizens lived in these concessions and settlements, where they had the same rights and privileges as other foreigners, including the protection of American law. America believed that this kind of encroachment on China should not be extended; but we also believed that when any encroachments were made, Americans were entitled to an equal footing in taking advantage of them. We worked quite freely within the framework of the imperialistic period, right up to Pearl Harbor. Mr. Grew's dispatches and diaries are striking evidence that our official concern was merely that no agreements extorted from China by Japan should diminish existing American privileges or exclude America from future opportunities.

The Open Door policy should always be thought

of as an Anglo-American policy. This is an important point, because there is a quite general tendency to think that Britain was one of the countries "stopped" by John Hay. As a matter of fact the ground was prepared for the Hay notes by Rockhill, later American Minister to China. A friend of John Hay, he worked closely with the British authorities. A great deal of the actual phrasing of the Open Door declaration was the work of an Englishman, Hippisley, a former member of the international, but predominantly British, staff which controlled the Chinese Customs, the principal source of revenue of the Chinese Government. The explanation is that the British held the strongest position in China. They preferred exploitation of China under a system of international privilege, working through such devices as the Treaty Ports, extraterritoriality, the control of the customs, and the right to maintain warships in Chinese territorial waters and to send them up the Yangtze River. If, however, there had been wide-open competition in annexing colonial possessions in China, the lion's share would have gone to the British lion. Therefore, when the British encouraged the Americans to initiate the Open Door policy, and then threw their own support heartily behind it, the matter was decided.

In this Anglo-American doctrine of "me too" lay hidden the flaw that fatally weakened our opposition to Japan's encroachments in China. *In the whole record of our protests to Japan, Britain and America never once contested Japan's right to make demands on China.* We only protested that privileges acquired by Japan should not exclude us.

In 1904–1905, at the time of the Russo-Japanese War, the Open Door doctrine was only a few years old, and had not yet acquired enough dignity and stability to make it free of the danger of being upset. All the Great Powers except Russia were distant from China and approached China by sea routes. It was comparatively easy for them to agree on the "rules of the game" in their competitive exploitation of China. Russia alone had a land approach to China, and consequently there was always the latent risk that Russia might upset the rules of the game by using her army to create some situation which could not be handled by the navies of America and Europe.

In such a situation it was felt that Japan might develop into a good watchdog against Russia. A good watchdog might well be considered entitled to a good kennel in South Manchuria, right on Russia's doorstep, even though South Manchuria was Chinese territory. American popular sentiment supported national policy, because Japan was thought of as a country which could be useful and would never be dangerous, and because the Tsar was never popular in this country and the tsarist system of political exile in Siberia was decidedly unpopular. It was therefore easy for President Theodore

Roosevelt to come forward as the mediator in peace negotiations between Japan and Russia at Portsmouth, New Hampshire, which resulted in better terms than Japan was entitled to in view of the fact that the military victory was not decisive.

America's willingness to make special allowances for Japan reached its peak in 1917, in the Lansing-Ishii exchange of notes. One paragraph of Lansing's note reads: "The Governments of the United States and Japan recognize that territorial propinquity creates special relations between countries, and, consequently, the Government of the United States recognizes that Japan has special interests in China, particularly in that part to which her possessions are contiguous." While it is true that in 1923, "in the light of the understanding arrived at by the Washington Conference," the agreement was canceled and made "of no further force or effect,"[4] it is also true that from the Mukden Incident in 1931 to Pearl Harbor in 1941 many Americans who found business with Japan profitable continued to argue on Japan's behalf that Japan had valid special interests arising out of contiguity to China.

Four major results of the Washington Conference require brief interpretative comment.

1. Britain abandoned the Anglo-Japanese alliance. This indicated that, European problems sup-

[4] For quotation of original text, see G. Nye Steiger, *A History of the Far East*, Boston, 1936, pp. 765–766, 802 *note* 1.

posedly settled, power should be projected into Asia from Europe and America, and should not be projected from overstrong bases within Asia. It relieved a deep American uneasiness about the alliance between Japan, holding a beachhead position in Asia, and Britain, whose policy apart from this alliance had long been relatively close to that of America.

2. Japan withdrew from Shantung. This reaffirmed the assumption that Japan's proper function (except in Manchuria) was to act as a junior partner in a system of treaties, privileges, controls, and safeguards, dominated by Britain and America, by which China was partly propped up and partly nailed down. Japan ought not to set up short-range controls interfering with the Anglo-American long-range controls.

3. Britain, America, and Japan agreed not to fortify certain strategic points. This was at the stipulation of Japan, and was the Japanese price for the abrogation of the Anglo-Japanese alliance.

4. A naval ratio was established of 5 for America, 5 for Britain, and 3 for Japan. The British and American calculation was that Japan, with the smaller ratio, would not be able to emerge aggressively from her corner of the Pacific but would be safeguarded by the inability of America and Britain to intervene easily in Japanese home waters. The Japanese calculation was that Britain and America would honor the nonfortification agreement men-

tioned under the preceding point. Japan would not. By combining secret fortification of bases with adroit use of her navy, Japan would in fact be able to build up an offensive potential offsetting the intentions of the 5–5–3 ratio.

Russia, although holding an important geographical position in Asia and on the Pacific, was not invited to the conference. Two assumptions were involved in this exclusion: –

1. The Soviet order would not survive, and Russia's place in Asia and on the Pacific should be discussed only with whatever government succeeded the Soviet order.

2. Russia, like Japan, should be kept from projecting into Eastern Asia, at close geographical range, any influence prejudicial to the long-range Anglo-American system of world power.

It is not surprising that a generation whose thought and indeed whose instinctive behavior was based on such assumptions failed to develop a body of experts who could explain to the American public what was going on in Asia. Our thinking about Asia stemmed from the great age of navigation at the beginning of the sixteenth century, when the old caravan routes were superseded by new sea routes. We still divide Asia into Near East, Middle East, India, Southeast Asia, and the Far East. We do so because we habitually think of approaching different sectors of Asia by different sea routes and because trade, colonial conquest, and political influence used to be projected into each of these sectors from points on its coast.

We now need to think of Asia not as a number of scattered regions to be approached by sea, or even by air, but as a vast, continuous area, within which communications by road, rail, and air, and industrial production, distribution, and consumption, can be developed on a scale not surpassed by that of North America.

The old formula represents only half of an equation; the half which expresses a historical lag, the continuing but diminishing influence of old factors in a new situation. For the new half of the equation we must work out a formula applicable to the longest land frontier in the world, curving for thousands of miles from Vladivostok to the Black Sea.

On one side of this frontier there is only one state, the Soviet Union; but the most important of its substates, which have a frontier in common with one or more foreign countries, have recently been granted the right of independent diplomatic representation and action. The complex populations of these substates, though full citizens of the Soviet Union, differ ethnically, linguistically, and culturally from the Russians and often have close traditional affiliations in non-Soviet territory adjacent to the Soviet frontier. On the other side of the frontier there are many totally different states containing many different peoples and cultures; but every single one of them also has linguistic and other ties with some part of the Soviet population.

Somewhere between the inland, Soviet frontier of Asia and the many coastal sectors of Asia, there is a new balance to be struck. Not a static balance, but a balance of forces, maintaining poise but allowing for change. The main forces entering into the balance will be: —

1. The retentive power of imperialism. We are already entitled to hope that the age of imperialism is over, in the sense that imperialism no longer has the power to increase its territorial spread. Imperialism, however, will recede unevenly, and in parts of the colonial world it will recede more slowly than many people have hoped. Moreover, even after the imperial structure has been dismantled some of the historical effects of imperialism will endure a long, long time.

2. A spread of Western democracy, which is permeated with capitalist thought. Some countries will quickly take over the political structure of democracy. Others will be strongly influenced by the thought of democracy, but will take on its political structure only slowly or only in part.

3. A comparable spread, especially in the interior of Asia, of the Soviet form of democracy, which is permeated with Marxist thought. As in the case of capitalist democracy, the rate of spread and the degree of influence will be uneven.

Of course there are many who deny the possibility of such a thing as a form of democracy molded by Marxist thought. Whatever our own opinion of the Soviet form of society, however, we must accommodate ourselves to the fact that there are others who consider it democratic, because they are allowed to integrate themselves with it, instead of being subordinated to it as colonial subjects. For well over a hundred years we have taken for granted the ascendancy of capitalist thought as *the* civilized mode of thought. Countries which escaped colonial subjection were accorded our esteem, and built up their own self-esteem, largely according to their success in adopting the thought and institutions of capitalism. Even in colonial countries we measured progress and prosperity not only by the spread of the capitalist enterprises of the ruling nation but also by the spread of capitalist thought among the subject people.

Capitalist ascendancy of this kind is no longer unchallenged. Marxist thought is now as fluently and cogently expressed in such Asiatic languages as Buryat-Mongol, Kazakh, Uzbek, and Tajik as it is in Russian or Ukrainian, because Marxist thought has rooted itself as firmly in the minds of these peoples as it has in the minds of the Russians and Ukrainians. In most territories adjoining the Soviet frontier Marxist thought cannot be dismissed as merely "subversive propaganda." It is no longer subversive, but competitive. Almost everywhere in these territories the old, indigenous ways of thought have lost some degree of prestige. In some of them capitalist thought has long held high prestige, even when it was resisted, or accepted only in part. Marxist thought, although it also meets resistance, is now gaining rapidly in prestige because of the growth of the Soviet Union into an immensely powerful state.

Problems of the industrialization of China and the rest of Asia, now so fashionable, should be considered in the light of the fact that industrialization is no longer identified with the unchallenged prestige of capitalist thought. The prestige of Soviet industrial production has increased with every victory won by weapons made in Soviet factories; and this prestige extends to the system of production as well as to the things produced. Along the inland frontier of Asia we may expect to see Soviet engineers increasingly consulted where formerly the only engineers consulted were European or American. If we are politically intelligent, we shall expect the Soviet engineers to be consulted on the organization and management of production as well as the design of machines and the layout of factories. We may count on seeing, over wide areas, the partial acceptance of Marxist ideas and the adoption of one or another part of the Soviet system.

What, then, will be America's primary concern with Asiatic problems? I shall be dealing with the

American interest under a number of topics; but here, in this opening chapter, there is a preliminary point which I want to make clear.

We cannot assume that Americans can draw authoritative blueprints for Asia. We cannot assume that Asia will follow some course ideally suitable to us. We are powerful enough – if we prove skillful enough – to influence Asia; but there are also strong tendencies for things to happen in Asia whether we want them to or not. Our relation to Asia is reciprocal. If Asia is a problem to us, we are also a problem to Asia. Americans do not remember this nearly often enough.

I can illustrate very simply what I mean. At the time of the United Nations conference on financial policy at Bretton Woods in July 1944, many American newspapers editorially criticized the views of the United States and British Treasuries. The tone of the criticism was indicated by the saying: "Bankers of the world, unite! You have nothing to lose but your Keynes!" Now China, and a number of other countries, are unable even to think of how they are going to tackle their economic problems except in terms of the probabilities and potentialities of American loans, investments, credits, and trade policies. Therefore, if they see a battle shaping up between the American Government, represented by the Treasury, and private financial interests speaking through the press, they must hold up their own planning and thinking until the internal decision in America is clear.

In this sense America is a very real problem to Asia; and the American problem and the Asiatic problem interact. If certain key solutions are not reached in America, corresponding solutions in Asia will be delayed. The situation in Asia is such that we cannot lightly cause delay in beginning to tackle major problems. Delay would cause dislocations of our own economic and political interests. America must realize that Asiatic problems are not academic. They work out to a plus or minus in American exports, imports, jobs – or breadlines, because unless we do our share in developing markets in Asia for what we produce, as well as in Europe, Latin America, and Africa, we shall not be able to employ all the men who should do the producing. An American policy toward Asia is therefore not a luxury but a domestic, American necessity.

CHAPTER II

JAPAN, THE EXPONENT OF CUT-RATE IMPERIALISM

WASHINGTON is full of experts who will tell you that the Japanese are mysterious, fanatical, and not to be understood by any ordinary use of the intellect. The same experts are also addicted to citing bits of lore which, they tell you condescendingly, explain why the Japanese always do this or never do that. In London, you can turn up just as many of these experts. The awe in which we hold them is remarkable. Somehow, nobody ever successfully challenges the racket. And yet, confused though the record of our experts on China is, the record of our Japan experts is even more fantastic. Probably at the end of the war it will turn out that some of the most true, devoted, unquestioning, esoteric initiates of the Japanese Emperor cult have been holding jobs in the United States Army, Navy, Marine Corps, and State Department, all the time. The same thing holds true for the Japanese Liberals cult, the Samurai Spirit cult, and a number of other hidden mysteries.

A crosslight can be thrown on our expert thinking by two quotations from Sumner Welles's *The Time for Decision.* On the subject of the Japanese invasion of Manchuria in 1931 Mr. Welles writes, on page 278: ". . . Neither the Department of State nor American representatives in the Far East had, prior to the invasion, any accurate or realistic conception of Japan's true intentions. Yet all during the summer months Japanese military officials had been blatantly frank about their intentions, and the extent of their military preparations had been by no means concealed. The United States was caught by surprise in spite of these warnings."

On page 294 Mr. Welles writes: "There is no foreign post where it is more difficult for an American Ambassador to learn the truth than Tokyo. The reports of Ambassador Grew from the outset of his mission to the last days – seen in the light of the present – reflected with amazing accuracy the true trend of events." [1]

Evidently it made little difference whether our condition were one of being negligently uninformed or one of being well-informed but inhibited in some way from applying our knowledge. Neither information nor lack of information was really pertinent to our minds, because our thinking was governed by a number of conventions. Such facts as came our way had to be fitted to the conventions.

[1] Welles, Sumner, *The Time for Decision,* Harper and Bros., 1944. This is a little too laudatory. See the footnote on pages 5–6.

If they did not match up with them, they were either ignored, or evaluated wrongly, or not evaluated in time. Even the "amazing accuracy" attributed to Ambassador Grew only became evident "in the light of the present."

And the old conventions continue to govern our habitual thinking about Japan. They are the sacred cows of our cheaper Japan-expert Brahmins. Without the cows, the Brahmins would not be revered, and without the Brahmins the cows would not be sacred. We shall never be able to treat the cows as cows if we continue to admit the authority of the Brahmins, and we shall never shake the authority of the Brahmins unless we stick to the point that a cow is a cow and the hell with sanctity.

Sacred Cow Number One, and in fact the cow to end all cows, is the Japanese Emperor. If we can make sense of him, there is nothing left of the legend that things Japanese are incomprehensible to the Western mind. Does the cult of the emperor mean the same thing to Japanese generals, admirals, directors of banks and corporations, factory workers, and peasants in the fields? Should America advocate the removal of the emperor as a focus of militarism, or support him as a focus of anti-militarism? Would a democratic monarchy be workable with a Japanese emperor at the apex? Where do the Japanese liberals belong in our political thinking? To what extent is it true that ideas originating outside of Japan are incomprehensible to Japanese minds, and ideas originating inside Japan incomprehensible to our minds? Some of these questions will be dealt with in a later chapter on American policy, but it is well to raise them here because at one point or another they touch the great emperor hoax.

The orthodox "expert" approach to the position of the emperor in Japan is all too often weakened by accepting the premise that in Japan the emperor is officially holy. This obliges the experts to pursue through the rabbit warren of history, literature, and Shintoism the rabbity questions of how holy the emperor is, and in what ways the idea of this holiness works in the minds of Japanese. To submit to such restrictions is as unscientific as it would be to limit oneself to a purely doctrinal investigation of such a complicated and sophisticated idea as that of the Holy Trinity, abandoning the resources of religious history and comparative religion. Moreover it is unnecessary. The truth is that the emperor can be taken out of the shadows of mystery by analyzing recent Japanese history as a whole. We are as free to use our common sense about Japan as about any other nation; and if we do, it is not at all impossible to understand the main structure of modern Japan, including the position of the emperor.

About a hundred years ago, soon after Perry opened Japan, a group within the Japanese people staved off foreign conquest by effecting their own quick and crushing conquest of the nation. By this conquest they brought their countrymen within the orbit of Western trade and Western political conventions even more effectively than if Japan had been made a colony; and it was this that made colonial conquest unnecessary.

Internal conquest of this kind in Japan was possible because the internal balance of Japanese society in the middle of the nineteenth century happened to be so poised that the shock administered by Perry's squadron, although not strong enough to shatter Japan's cohesion, was strong enough to throw control into the hands of a group that was well equipped to seize and use control. This group was one which had developed under the crust of the Tokugawa government. It was not opposed to the kind of power which the Tokugawa had, but hungry to appropriate that power.

For two and a half centuries Japan had been under the Tokugawa Shogunate. The Shogunate was a peculiar institution of centralized feudalism. The emperor reigned, but did not rule. The shogun was interposed between him and the nation. Like the emperor himself and all feudal nobles, the shoguns held their dictatorial powers by hereditary right. The office in this period was held by the Tokugawa family; but this family was an offshoot of the Minamoto group of clans, each of which was descended from the son of an emperor.

A very brief explanation of a few Japanese terms is advisable at this point – if only because such terms are frequently used to thicken unnecessarily the fog of legend about Japan. The following definitions have been made as simple as possible, and it should be remembered that full definition would involve a great deal of detail and qualification, because in Japan, as in Europe, feudal terms meant somewhat different things at different periods.

Shogun: Originally a general. In the Middle Ages, when the frontier between the Japanese and the Ainu aborigines still ran right across the main island of Japan, the position of commander in chief against the Ainu was an important feudal post. Out of this military function there developed the political function of the shogun as a kind of hereditary feudal prime minister. Eventually the shogun usurped most of the real power of the emperor. There were, of course, similar but not identical tendencies in feudal Europe.

Daimyo: A great noble, corresponding to those European feudal nobles who were powerful enough to be the real rulers of their territories. Nominally the power and privileges of a daimyo were delegated to him by the emperor.

Samurai: Gentry, who like the feudal gentry of Europe ranged from lesser nobles down to squires. A samurai owned allegiance to a daimyo. Sometimes he owned land and was protected by the daimyo, who in return could summon him to arms at any time. Other samurai, who had ceased to own land, still owed armed service and received in return a stipend, paid in grain or computed by the value of the grain, showing that originally land and rank went together.

Ronin: A masterless warrior who had renounced or been released from his samurai allegiance to a daimyo.

Although the Tokugawa shoguns, like earlier shoguns of other clans, were legally sanctioned in their office by grant or decree of the emperor, they had in fact won their position by success in feudal wars between the great noble clans of Japan. These were not civil wars which attempted to change the political order; they were purely competitive wars between rivals aspiring to dominance within an unchanging system of power. The Tokugawa clan had laid its grasp on power in the great battle of Sekigahara, in 1600. To make its hold permanent, the clan relied on two policies: –

1. It set up a capital at Yedo, later known as Tokyo or "Eastern Capital," at a distance from Kyoto, the emperor's capital. The shogun was interposed completely between the emperor and the business of government by the requirement that all feudatories should sign a written oath of loyalty to the shogun.

2. The feudatories were divided into two classes: those who had fought on the side of the Tokugawa clan before the battle of Sekigahara, and those who had submitted only after that battle. Distinctions of privilege between these two groups were intended

to ensure that the early allies of the Tokugawa would always be on the watch against any dangerous growth of power among the "outer" clans whose allegiance had been given under compulsion.

Under this rigid structure of power the emperor remained ritualistically the source which conferred a sanction on the real power held by the shogun. In spite of this venerability, however, neither the common people nor the nobles who enjoyed real power worked very hard at venerating him. The prevailing attitude toward the emperor was a good deal like that of the many Christians who believe that of course God exists and religion is a good thing, but rarely go to church.

By the time that Perry sailed into Yedo Bay in 1853 no society in Europe or Asia could compare with that of Japan in the completeness and tenacity of its feudal outlook and feudal institutions. In 1641 seclusion from foreign contact had finally been enforced, except for a few carefully watched and strictly circumscribed Dutch and Chinese at Nagasaki, and for about two hundred and fifty years the Tokugawa shoguns had devoted themselves to the sole principle of maintaining and perpetuating feudal institutions.

Nevertheless, there was great internal pressure in Japan. The Tokugawa and the "inner" clans most closely associated with them had, in the course of enjoying their privileges, become largely attached to cities in which they could spend their wealth. By doing so, they nourished merchants who gradually raised the importance of wealth in money to a level at which it could compete, as a social and political sanction, with aristocratic birth and revenue in grain from landed estates. The urbane English historian, Sansom, beautifully describes how the feudal standard of revenue from the land in grain interacted with the merchant standard of revenue from profit on the turnover of capital. Markets and prices were upset and all values confused to the point where some samurai surrendered their social privileges for the sake of economic advantage, while on the other hand so many prosperous merchants were attracted by the traditional prestige of an aristocratic connection that there came to be "a regular tariff for the entry of a commoner into a samurai family."[2]

While these changes were undermining the cohesion of the Tokugawa and their close adherents, the older feudalism remained relatively vigorous among the great lords of the "outer" clans, the most important of which were grouped in Southwestern Japan. They had an unimpaired feudal control over their own retainers and peasants, whereas change had grown up slowly around the Tokugawa until it embarrassed them like heavy ivy on an old oak.

From these outer clans came most of the men who conquered Japan from within, with the result

[2] Sansom, G. B., *Japan: A Short Cultural History.* D. Appleton-Century, New York, 1931, p. 514.

that the "new" Japan of the Meiji Era (1868–1912) was founded by men whose minds were colored by the strongest feudal traditions in the society of old Japan.

Commodore Perry showed the warriors of Japan that Western countries had the ships, the weapons, and the methods to conquer Japan if once they determined to do so – a revelation which gave the most daring men in the outer clans an opportunity to overthrow the Tokugawa Shogunate and conquer their own country under the guise of saving Japan from foreign conquest.

One of the earlier modern authorities on Japan points out that "fifty-five individuals may be said to have planned and carried out the overthrow of the Yedo administration" – the shogunate. Of these only eight were nobles of the emperor's own court, who had titles but not territory. Five were territorial nobles of the daimyo class. The remaining forty-two were from families of lesser rank or wealth among the samurai of the outer clans. "The average age of the whole did not exceed thirty." [3]

The decisive group belonged to a class which had enough to lose to be fundamentally conservative, and enough to gain to be willing to risk bold experiments. They were born at a high enough level in feudal society to be not diffident about taking the lead; at a low enough level to be ambitious. In

[3] Captain Frank Brinkley, article "Japan" in *Encyclopaedia Britannica*, 11th ed., 1911.

age, they stood below the heads of clans who were hesitant in the face of strange, new emergencies. In class, they stood at the level where the demands of the great broke down in transmission to peasants, commoners, and townsmen. They were in touch both with the giving of orders and with the evasion of orders. To such men, at certain junctures in history, there comes the opportunity to arrogate to themselves the giving of orders, combined with the knowledge of how to see that those orders are executed and not evaded.

The story of the "revolution" against the shogunate, quickly consolidated as a counterrevolution under the Meiji Era, is extraordinarily intricate. The main factors and phases can, however, be intelligibly summarized: –

1. The emperor was dug out of his innocuous desuetude and made a new focus of national loyalty combined with feudal loyalty. This made it possible for key men on the Tokugawa side to evade their feudal loyalty to the shogun on the excuse of a higher loyalty to the emperor. It also made possible a division of the spoils between the two major anti-Tokugawa clans of Satsuma and Choshu, which, if the shogunate had not been abolished, would have had to fight each other to see which clan should establish a new shogunate.

2. Unity in face of the foreigner was used as an appeal to effect a quick regrouping around the emperor. The new, confident young leaders dared to

train peasants in the use of firearms. With these troops they first crushed those of the sword-bearing samurai who were so quixotic that they could not tell the difference between an unprofitable windmill and a profitable new militarism. Then, by resorting to the new device of conscription, they used armed peasants to hold down unarmed peasants and made it possible for the bigger feudal nobles to continue as a privileged class of great landowners.

National conscription, enacted in 1872–1873 and revised in 1883, was used as a dam to prevent the peasants from breaking out in revolution. Since the dam backed up a great reservoir of peasant manpower, there had to be a spillway to ease the pressure. The spillway was expansion into the continent of Asia, the stages and timing of which became acute political issues from the beginning of the Meiji Era.[4]

In order to carry out their program, the men

[4] See E. H. Norman, *Soldier and Peasant in Japan: The Origins of Conscription*. New York, 1943. Also his earlier book, *Japan's Emergence as a Modern State*. New York, 1940. Widely read in Japanese sources, this young Canadian is already the most authoritative contemporary analyst of Japan's economy, society, and government. He is to some extent a disciple, and in a sense the successor, of Sir George Sansom, whose *Japan: A Short Cultural History*, unrivaled for its combination of learning, insight, and gentle wit, ends at the beginning of the Meiji Era.

who conquered Japan from within had to get there ahead of Western imperialism. The foreigners had already begun to impose controls over Japan in the form of extraterritorial rights and customs tariffs favoring cheap imports from abroad. To prevent these controls from being extended, the founders of modern Japan took the lead themselves in expanding trade.

More trade meant more wealth and power in the hands of those engaged in trade. A clash between trading interests and feudal interests was avoided by recourse to that eminently modern device, the merger. The "insiders" of the feudal group went into trade. Japan, an agrarian country, had a negligible accumulation of cash capital. The government, by using its power to tax, could raise capital to expand trade and industry rapidly, without coming under foreign economic control. In its use of this power, the government gave charters and subsidies in planned rotation to create and promote the necessary new economic activities. Thus the feudal class remained politically supreme, but what the feudal class did with its power was profitable to trade and industry. Because of this the new economic interests which might have competed with the old political interests became instead intertwined with them. Conversely, it was easy for men of samurai origin to enter banking, trade, and industry when these pursuits were made auxiliary to the interests of a government which was also of samurai derivation; and this was made even easier by cash grants from the government.

The emperor was brought into the team by the investment of "imperial household" funds in the new enterprises. In this way the emperor remained the ideological pillar of the feudal system and became at the same time a main pillar of vested interest in the new, capitalistic structure.

From the beginning, the development of an internal market was made subsidiary to the development of markets abroad for Japan's new products. Japan was deficient in coal, oil, and iron, the basic requirements of heavy industry and armaments. Japan had therefore to produce with the utmost cheapness, in order to pile up profit balances for the purchase of these requirements. The peasants had to be kept poor, so that surplus labor from the land would willingly enter factories at low wages; but this meant that neither peasants nor factory workers could buy the new factory products in large quantities.

In this way the Japanese who conquered Japan created a remarkable dual system, combining a highly cartelized industry with an agriculture which preserved the social outlook of feudalism. Capitalism treats agriculture as an activity in which capital can be invested. Feudalism draws tribute from the farmer, but does not invest capital in the land. In Japanese agriculture the tenant has duties, the landlord rights, under a sharecropping system which forces the tenant to pay tribute in order to be allowed to work the land. The landlord, being able to make would-be tenants compete against each other, is not under pressure to spend capital in modernizing the methods of agriculture; he simply assumes that the way to increase crops per acre is to increase the aches per cropper.

The peasants, therefore, became the draft animals dragging Japan's chariot of "remarkable progress" which admirers abroad were so ready to praise. To keep them docile, a number of devices were elaborated. Men were kept under social control by heavy indoctrination during military service. One part of their minds had to be made modern enough so that while in uniform they could efficiently handle the necessary weapons and machinery. Another part had to be kept feudal in outlook, so that after conscription they would return contentedly to the rice paddy and the fishing smack. It is impossible here to go into detail, though the details can frankly be called fascinating as a study in the manipulation of people. For instance, there was a deliberate screening out of students and urban workers in peacetime conscription, so as to keep the standing army heavily peasant-minded.

Women were kept under social control by the industrial barrack system. A girl in a textile mill would be indentured for a term of years, under a cash advance to her parents. Living in a barracks, she had the minimum contact with the urban mind.

She was fed and looked after well enough to prevent physical deterioration, and given enough education to make her a more nimble worker. "Education," however, had a strong emphasis on deportment and social attitude. As a result, she would eventually return to her rural home unaffected by her sojourn in the industrial age, meekly willing to accept a marriage arranged by her parents, and to accept also the fact that her surplus earnings would either be retained by her parents or be made over to her husband's family.

The success of Japan's rulers in exploiting feudal agriculture and mechanized industry has a bearing on two problems which puzzle Americans – Japan's overpopulation and the possibility of a future democratic Japan.

Japan's overpopulation is closely related to rural poverty and unmechanized farming. The farmer who has no capital and whose landlord refuses to invest capital and demands a heavy rent can only get more out of the land by putting more labor into it. Unable to hire labor, he must have children to help him; but when the children in turn have children, there are too many mouths for the land to support. In Tokugawa Japan the surplus was kept down by infanticide, grimly described in farming language as *mabiki*, "the word used of thinning a row of vegetables." [5] In modern Japan the surplus goes into the factories, but the constant rural over-

[5] Sansom, *op. cit.*, p. 508.

production of children keeps up the competition for jobs and keeps down wages. In the relatively liberal 1920's there was, not unnaturally, a tendency to limit families by birth control; but under the militarists the teaching of birth control is forbidden and the people are taught that large families are a social and patriotic duty.

This kind of overpopulation cannot be remedied by colonial conquest, as Japanese propaganda persuaded many Americans to believe. The only remedy is to raise social standards to a level where a woman is not a chattel and can refuse to serve simply as breeding stock, and to raise economic standards to the level where both farming and factory families can save money and can afford to have the children they want, without being forced to go on having children for the sake of child labor.

As for the problem of a future democracy in Japan, it is the fashion to say that the Japanese are incapable of understanding ideas alien to their own culture. The history of Japan, however, does not support the "almost fatuous dictum" that the East is unchanging.[6] In the sixteenth century, when the Japanese were living in a world of purely Oriental thought, Christianity spread rapidly among them, aided by "the desire of the great feudatories to derive profit from foreign trade" coming in with the ships which brought the missionaries. The extermination of the Christians less than a century

[6] *Ibid.*, p. 424.

later was also not a purely religious question. Both Christian nobles and Christian peasants fought in the feudal wars and peasant insurrections which ended in the triumph of the Tokugawa Shogunate, and the final stand of the Christians, when 37,000 were killed at the Castle of Shimabara in 1638, "was among the immediate causes" of the Tokugawa policy of seclusion.[7] The inference is clear: any system of thought or belief has both political and economic implications, in the "mysterious" East as in the "rational" West. The Japanese, like other people, can adopt any system of society; but only if the changes made go beyond catchwords and permeate the whole society. Democracy in Japan cannot be attained by changing the status of the emperor, but will require democratic changes throughout Japanese society.

There is in fact a democratic potential in Japanese life, which has had to be kept down by force. From 1931 onward, each crisis of Japanese policy has been preceded by attempts of the people to form democratic parties and to vote against war. The militarists have forced crises abroad partly in order to seize and keep control at home; and since, in these crises, they have always professed to be defending the interests of the emperor, the emperor is now identified as the resort of final appeal against any democratic trend. The democratic potential is still there, but if it is ever to emerge we must first,

[7] *Ibid.*, pp. 407, 408.

in the words of Sun Fo, "puncture the myth of the divinity of the Mikado." [8]

The indications of Japan's own history are borne out by the record of the Americans of Japanese ancestry, who have shown themselves capable of being Americans of the finest kind. They have been guilty of no sabotage either in Hawaii or on the Pacific Coast, and without their loyalty and labor in Hawaii the damage at Pearl Harbor could not have been repaired so quickly. Their military units in Italy are the most decorated in the American Army, and individuals on special duty in the Pacific have shown outstanding heroism. There is a lesson in the fact that the spirit shown has been better in Hawaii, where there is less economic and social discrimination, than among the Pacific Coast Japanese who have been the victims of deliberately incited and organized prejudice.[9] We have been extraordinarily stupid, as well as cruel, in not publicizing widely the American-ness of our fellow citizens of Japanese ancestry.

Military aggression was the only possible outcome of Japan's social system, and it will be renewed unless the Japanese are allowed to change the system. The whole structure was one of war. Such a

[8] Sun Fo, "The Mikado Must Go," *Foreign Affairs*, Oct. 1944, p. 23.

[9] For full documentation, see *Prejudice: Japanese-Americans: Symbol of Racial Intolerance*, by Carey McWilliams. Little, Brown and Co.

structure could not stand securely unless the Japanese flag flew over the sources of war materials; and as the war materials did not exist in sufficient quantities within the Japanese islands, access by trade to sources abroad had sooner or later to be converted into control of the sources abroad.

Because of our habitual thinking, we have failed to see how these interacting factors link the Japanese "liberals" (another sacred cow) and "militarists." It ought to have been a basic assumption instead of a shocking discovery "in the light of the present" (to pick up again Mr. Welles's perhaps unintentionally deadly phrase) that the opposition between militarism and Japan's commercial and industrial interests was only one of timing. Japan's trade profits paid a heavy tribute to build up a military and naval establishment powerful enough to seize raw material sources abroad if necessary.

If necessary – when? The liberals were those who hated to close the profitable period of preparation for war. The militarists were those who argued the advantages of each opportunity to convert preparation into execution. The militarists were professionally prone to argue that the hog had been fattened and was ready for slaughter. The liberals were professionally prone to urge that the hog would become even fatter if not killed quite yet.

This disagreement as to the timing of aggression – a very different thing from disagreement in principle as to the propriety of aggression — has been a thread running through all the recent history of Japan. It was exposed to view early in the "liberal" Meiji Era, and was never hidden after that. Japan adopted conscription in 1873, after acute controversy. Before conscription was adopted, the fire-eaters agitated for the conquest of Korea. They wanted a "samurai war" with the naked sword, and they were largely the men described by Norman as "the more obtuse and noisy (hence less dangerous) reactionaries" who were against conscription. The proponents of conscription were against the premature invasion of Korea, but they were not against conquest abroad. The only issue was whether to conquer Korea with swords or to wait, prepare, and do it later with guns.

The emperor was integral to the expansion of Japan, whether the trigger was pulled late or soon. Economically, he belonged with the liberals, because of his huge investments. Militarily, he belonged with the militarists, as the ritualistic fount of military morale. Socially, he belonged with both liberals and militarists because he was the keystone of the arch of economic and social privilege under which the people passed on their way to "work, obey, fight." [10] Our failure to identify the Japanese

[10] It is not surprising that it is difficult to document the wealth of the Japanese Emperor. The *Far East Year Book*, Tokyo, 1941, gives the following partial list of his industrial holdings in 1938: —

emperor with Japanese imperialism is akin to our failure to detect that timing, not principle, was what divided "liberals" from militarists. We shall never be able to draw up a rational policy toward Japan until we recognize that only revolution can solve the problem of the imperial institution in Japan. It is the institution that counts; the personal character or predilections of any individual emperor are more or less irrelevant.

It is a mistake to think that Japan could achieve "democratic monarchy" by reform. We Americans

---

Nippon Yusen Kaisha (shipping)	161,000 shares
Mitsui Bank	54,000 shares
Hypothec Bank	10,000 shares
Oji Paper	62,000 shares
South Manchuria Railway	38,000 shares
Tokyo Electric Light	24,000 shares
Bank of Japan	141,000 shares
Taiwan (Formosa) Sugar	40,000 shares

Perhaps more significant is the following description of the Emperor's legal ability to make use of his economic power, taken from the same source: "The ordinary civil or commercial law is applicable to the [imperial] property only when it does not conflict with the Imperial Household Law and the present law."

Shirosi Nasu, in his *Aspects of Japanese Agriculture*, New York, 1941, lists the following imperial land holdings in 1939: —

Forest	292,775,000 acres
Prairie	340,550 acres
Fit for paddy rice	22,596 acres
Fit for upland rice	56,220 acres

are likely to be misled by thinking of England as the example of a democratic monarchy. Because the English Revolution came before our own, and Cromwell is for us only a schoolbook figure of secondary importance, we are not aware of the ghost of King Charles I, who no longer needs to look over the shoulder of the occupant of the English throne, but is still there, behind the throne. One of the important reasons why the British can be democratic and have a king too is because, at a time which has now receded so far into history that it can be talked about without discomfort, the English people cut off the head of an English king. Until the Japanese people have done something equally progressive (whatever the suitable equivalent of cutting off heads may be), everybody will be uncomfortable and no palliative reform will be adequate.

We have also yet to recognize the fascist character of Japanese society, and to draw the proper conclusions. This problem has been muddled for us by people who talk of Japanese imitations of German methods and policies as if they merely conferred on Japan an appearance of fascism, or constituted an imitative, secondary fascism. The truth is that Japanese fascism is more deeply rooted than that of Germany. Nothing could be more quintessentially fascist than the Japanese phenomenon of a whole society of twentieth-century hands guided by medieval brains. So medieval was the texture of society in Japan when "modernization" began that the monstrosity of fascism could be created by keeping the minds of men and women unchanged, while introducing new technical skills for their hands.

Germany had to do the opposite; to retain the twentieth-century technical skills while turning the minds of her people back toward medievalism. The whole insane, obscene nightmare of Hitler, Rosenberg, "blood and soil," the "leader principle," the creation of elites, and the sadistic frenzy of anti-Semitism can with rough accuracy be called a synthetic feudalism, as compared with Japan's continuation of feudalism into the twentieth century. The difference between the two countries can be summed up in one especially interesting contrast: even stupid Nazis know that they have been taught, indoctrinated; but many intelligent Japanese do not know that their minds have been shaped for them, because the conditioning to which they are subjected is the continuation of a process begun long ago.

At this point it is advisable to look into the record of America's connection with the rise of modern Japan. We find two traditional themes in American writing about Japan: dislike of the competitor, leading to somewhat random accusations of unfair methods and sinister ambitions; and sympathy for a fellow competitor whose interests were in some ways closer to ours than those of more powerful competitors. In expressing either like or dislike, our vocabulary, like our thought, was largely political. It did not range into a deep searching of social trends because we ourselves were playing our part in an age of imperialism.

In the circumstances it was natural even for Americans who studied Japanese, and even for those who grew up in Japan, to accept Japanese explanations of Japan's history, politics, and economic problems. Moreover the average American who seriously studied Japan was, because of his own social position and income, in touch chiefly with the upper middle class; and the upper middle class in every country has its own conceptions, preconceptions, and misconceptions about its own country, as has become uncomfortably obvious in recent years.

Americans, and Europeans too, in taking over the views and explanations offered to them by *some* Japanese, habitually made the mistake of thinking that they were getting *the* right answers from *the* Japanese. It is no wonder that the more rounded knowledge of a Sansom and the more deeply penetrating observations of a Norman were altogether exceptional. Nor is it surprising that the post-revolutionary Russians, coming on the scene with fresh minds, or at least with preconceptions quite different from ours, were often right in stressing a number of phenomena whose importance we underestimated; although the Russians too, trained in European concepts of "class warfare," made their mistakes in analyzing the society of Japan.[11]

After the defeat of Germany in 1918 Americans who thought of Japan as a dangerous competitor began to outnumber Americans who thought of Japan as a legitimate competitor and profitable customer. By that time, however, Japan had perfected a remarkable technique which can best be described as cut-rate imperialism. Continuing to work within the system of international treaties as a competitor in China, Japan also went beyond competition and set to work to eliminate the power of Britain and America from Eastern Asia.

A number of devices were used in combination: —

1. Abuse of the right of political asylum was one of the defects of the extraterritorial system. Chinese war lords and corrupt politicians who had made their pile would retire to Hong Kong or Dairen, or to a foreign concession or international

[11] See O. Tanin and E. Yohan, *Militarism and Fascism in Japan,* New York, 1934, and *When Japan Goes to War,* New York, 1936. There has been considerable controversy over theories about Japan among Soviet authorities. Both Tanin and Yohan have been purged, or at least have ceased to publish. In 1937 the important journal *Tikhii Okean* (*Pacific Ocean*) was rebuked for overestimating the strength of military fascism in Japan and underestimating the potential popular resistance to it. It is unfortunate that there is not a wider selection of Russian comment on Japan available in translation, because its general average is high.

settlement, put their money in a foreign bank, under a foreign flag, and live in security. Japanese militarists, especially agents of the Kwantung Army, like Doihara, improved on this: they encouraged and financed Chinese adventurers to use Japanese concessions as bases in which to plan civil wars and from which to sally out on trouble-making expeditions. When disorder resulted, the Japanese came forward as loyal supporters of the international system of "law and order," strengthening their military forces on the spot and appealing to the common interest of Britain and America in law and order.

2. The precedents built up in this way were skillfully used at the time of the fighting in Shanghai in 1932 and again in 1937. The Japanese found useful support from local British and American interests for the claim that the Japanese forces, using a part of the International Settlement as a beachhead for an attack on the Chinese City of Shanghai, were only trying, in their blunt way, to secure "law and order"; while the Chinese, by resisting, were endangering the "neutrality" of the Settlement.

3. The confusion which they created in China was also exploited by the Japanese in another way. Foreign enterprise interested in China was urged to think of the advantages of investing in Japan instead. Let Americans count on Japan as a reliable country – expanding, of course, but steady and strong. Japan wanted investment money, not risk

money. Let the Americans invest in Japan. The Japanese themselves would undertake enterprises in China in which there would be, for Americans, too much risk. Being closer to Asia, knowing Asia better, and being able and ready to apply disciplinary pressure when needed, the Japanese would be able to make profit enough for themselves and enough more to pay the interest on American investments in Japan.

Japan made a mistake in attacking us at Pearl Harbor. We should not let this mistake wipe out the memory of our own mistakes. By the time of Pearl Harbor, the Japanese had thoroughly undermined the international system of "law and order," extraterritoriality, concessions, and privileged economic activity in which we and they had for so long been partners. Through this partnership the privileged nations had held an advantage over China; but the system provided no method of control when one partner, Japan, used legality for lawless purposes. American policy in the Far East had lost all drive and originality. We had no policy except to appeal to statutes of law and order; we had no intention to create the realities of law and order and had never made up our minds at what point to stand and defend law and order.

With this in mind, we should not deceive ourselves with too much smug self-approval for having abandoned extraterritoriality in China *after* Pearl Harbor. We abandoned something that no longer worked, partly because we had not made it work. We abandoned something that we would not have been able to restore. The policy decision was one that required little decisiveness of the mind. That leaves us with a problem for the future which requires real thought and real decision. The age of imperialism, though not dead, is withering. The decades of drift are over. We must now set a course. Have we any idea what course to set?

CHAPTER III

REVOLUTION AND NATIONALISM IN CHINA

NINETEENTH-CENTURY China was different from Japan in one all-important respect. There was no group capable of unifying the country by internal conquest. The imperial dynasty, which was of Manchu origin, could not create Chinese nationalism. Chinese landlordism had many feudal characteristics, but the landlords themselves were a "scholar gentry" with no military feudalism in their tradition.

China escaped conquest partly because of rivalry between the nations which might have divided her territory, partly because outright territorial conquest was giving way to new, more indirect methods of imperialism. Within limits, representatives of the imperial court and government were able to play one foreign government off against another, but even this field of maneuver was restricted when foreign diplomatic representatives presented their demands to China in a body instead of individually.

In such a situation, new leadership in China had

to be revolutionary and had to be directed both against the government and against the entrenched foreign interests which had indirect control over the government. Foreigners in China in 1911 almost universally failed to understand this. The more intelligent foreigners were in favor of reform but they thought of reform in terms of stronger, more honest administrators who would make the government work better. They did not appreciate the extent to which the government had become identified with foreign treaty privileges limiting the sovereignty of China and the powers and functions of the government.

To the minds of most foreigners in China, anything that went beyond the program of administrative reform was not realism but "extremism." When events proved that reform always broke down, the extraterritorially protected Treaty Port foreigners, concerned primarily with the perpetuation of their vested interests, merely retreated from political analysis to political mythology. According to this mythology, "the people of China" were congenitally incompetent in politics. All they really wanted was law and order under a strong government which would cut down corruption and not tax too heavily. The natural symbol of such a government was a revered emperor. Therefore, the really "progressive" policy was to strengthen the imperial administration with as many foreign advisors and special commissioners as possible, to maintain a stiff front with gunboats and garrisons against "irresponsible mobs," and to give "idealists and dreamers" a rough brush-off.

Faced with this combination of cold power and stony incredulity, more and more sober, hard-headed, businesslike Chinese became "extremists" and "visionaries," providing an urban upper class revolutionary leadership. In the earlier phases the successful Chinese merchant or banker would contribute to secret revolutionary societies and help an ardent apostle of revolution like Sun Yat-sen, even if he were still afraid to show his own hand openly, because he was impatient of his own government and resentful of foreign privilege both as a Chinese and as a merchant or banker. Foreign merchants trading in China were not subject to Chinese taxation. China's tariff, imposed by treaty, made the importation of foreign goods so cheap that Chinese enterprise was hampered in building up home industries. Foreign banks could actually issue their own notes, in Chinese currency values. And while honest Chinese money had to compete under a handicap, dishonest Chinese money, looted by war lords or grafted by corrupt officials, could always find a refuge in foreign banks. The honest and able Chinese merchants and bankers and industrialists were forced to decide that they must work for a new kind of Chinese government which would mobilize enough strength to force the foreigners to loosen their stranglehold.

Chinese abroad were even more enthusiastic in the cause of revolution. While foreigners in China had more than equality, Chinese abroad had less than equality. In America and other countries they were denied naturalization. In the colonial countries they were treated on a level with the subject peoples. A number of poor Chinese had become successful and wealthy in the colonies; but the money that they had made conferred no rights on them. To take their money back to China was no solution. In making it, they had learned ways of doing things that were not the ways of the old China. Only a new China could give them scope for the kinds of things they had learned to do, new opportunities of investment for setting their money to work, and political rights which, as they very well knew, were a necessary complement to their economic abilities. Even if they were to stay abroad, only a new China could give them the assurance enjoyed by citizens of a country with equality of status.

Westerners, impatient of the "antics of hot-headed boys," were slow to appreciate the key importance of students in Chinese colleges in giving a real impetus to the revolutionary movement. They represented a class of unique importance in the social structure of China, and in the decades between 1911 and 1931 they represented successive generations coming of age at a time of crisis in their country's history.

Throughout Chinese history a few men, if they had luck in addition to brains, have always been able to rise from the humblest origins to the highest posts, by passing the state examinations and proving their abilities in office. But the democratic value of the Chinese respect for education and brains has frequently been overestimated. In practice, the sons of leisure families had an advantage in the intense and protracted study needed to pass examinations, since the study was of a kind in which a private tutor was almost a necessity. In an overwhelmingly agricultural country like China, the sons of landlords inevitably outnumbered all others in higher education. Under the old order it was they who became the mandarins.

As the influence of foreigners increased, the faster a Chinese rose to be a high official the sooner he came to the level at which he was called on the carpet by foreign officials and representatives, to provide for satisfying a foreign demand, to make good some deficiency which had brought down a foreign protest. Moreover, the traditional system of Chinese education was breaking down. The government itself saw that it was necessary to introduce modern schools, in which foreign subjects were taught in foreign languages, especially English. It was the able student whose mind was both fed and aroused by these changing conditions. He might not have experience and maturity, but his intelligence told him that he must either use his training to free his country from the foreign control intertwined with the imperial system, or meekly serve the foreign domination of China. His youth gave him the ardor to make the patriotic choice, and his partly foreign schooling brought him into sympathy with the new businessmen who also stood partly outside of the traditional system, because, in making their money in the new ways, they were daily forced by the system of unfair privilege to make a dollar for the foreigner before they could make half a dollar for themselves.

Naturally, when all of these factors first began to work together, there were always those who would rather serve the foreigner than risk losing the half dollar. There were always those who would not refuse an immediate post in a subservient government to work for the ideal of a future post in an independent government. Nevertheless, as modern education spread and wealth grew, even those who dared not show themselves in the revolutionary movement would act only inefficiently and reluctantly to impede it.

In the history of the Chinese Revolution, changes in the composition of the following are even more important than changes in the leadership. By the time that Sun Yat-sen died, in 1925, the ideas and methods of organization developed by the middle-class nationalist leaders had spread out among the people as a whole. Once this stage was reached, periods in which the revolutionary movement was controlled by its leaders began to alternate with periods in which the leaders were pushed ahead by the demands of their followers. There was an early enthusiasm for revolution among men who, like the leaders, had been partly detached by changing conditions from the old ways of thinking and of doing things – soldiers and underofficers, workers on the new railways and steamships, and in the new mines and mills and factories, employees in government offices of a new type, like the Post Office, which had ramifications all over the country but which did not, in its daily routine, inculcate the mental habits of the bureaucratic underling of the old type. Many of these people, especially the soldiers and unskilled laborers, were of peasant origin, and from them the idea of revolution with a new purpose eventually spread back among the peasants and took root among them. The new revolutionary ideas were quickly understood by the peasants, who already had a tradition of rebellion against misgovernment. Indeed, Sun Yat-sen himself had been influenced by the traditions of the great Taiping Rebellion of the mid-nineteenth century; it was part of the peasant background which gave him a stronger instinct for action, and a deeper faith in the common people, than most of the Western-educated intellectuals.

We can, therefore, mark off the course of the Chinese Revolution into phases. Each phase had a double aspect: a partial increase in the cohesion of

China, and a partial loosening of the foreign grip. Each phase was greeted, at the outset, by cries of bloody murder from the foreign vested interests in China – which had great influence with their consular and diplomatic representatives on the spot and their governments at home – protesting that all the values of law, order, property, and society were being subverted, and that chaos threatened. Each phase closed with a partial softening of Chinese demands, in order to consolidate major gains by making minor concessions, and with tentative acceptance by some foreigners, merging into grudging acquiescence among all foreigners.

Although the foreigners in China had uniform rights and privileges, they did not have uniform interests. There were always a few who saw a chance of gaining an advantage over their competitors by being a little bit ahead in coming to terms with the Chinese with whom they did business. On the whole, newcomers looking for new kinds of business were quicker to yield than the old-timers whose interests were vested in the old order. For this reason American enterprise tended to be more liberal than British enterprise, and led the way in dealing with independent Chinese businessmen, while the British clung more stubbornly to the old system of the "compradore," the Chinese agent and go-between tied to a particular foreign enterprise by a bond or cash deposit to guarantee his honesty.

There were also differences, moreover, between firms under the same flag. Those which dealt entirely in the Treaty Ports were the most conservative, especially those which enjoyed monopolies or near-monopolies, like the shipping interests. Other firms imported foreign commodities like cotton goods in the old days, and later oil, sugar, or dyestuffs, and were anxious to expand the market for them far into the interior. One such commodity could create a chain with many links of trade. A Chinese merchant in the interior would make himself the agent for several commodities. Receiving consignments of these, he would sell them on the local market. Then, instead of remitting the cash, he would buy wool, cotton, peanuts, furs, or other export goods and consign them to a Treaty Port — often creating a subsidiary chain of deals. In this way he took a margin of profit both in selling and in buying. Foreign firms whose own profits were linked with the profits of these Chinese enterprises were often quick to see the advantages of an independent class of Chinese merchants, financed by their own banking methods.

The Chinese also had their own divisions and oppositions. Chinese in the shipping business, for instance, were severely handicapped by foreign privilege. The general rule among sovereign countries is to permit no coastal trade and no river trade under foreign flags. In China, however, "treaty power" ships had the right to sail as they liked, under their own flags, between Chinese coastal ports and up the great Yangtze waterway, reaching into the heart of China. The small and struggling Chinese merchant marine, in order to compete with them, had to resort to low wages, poor working conditions, and dangerous overcrowding and overloading.

Under such competitive conditions it might be expected that Chinese shipowners would oppose the formation of seamen's unions, demanding better pay and working conditions. In 1922 the Chinese Seamen's Union fought and won a famous strike at Hong Kong which was both a landmark in the early history of labor organization in China and a triumph of the political revolutionary movement. The strike showed what organized labor could do to win concessions from employers, but it was widely approved by Chinese employers because it was directed primarily against the British shipping interests.

Chinese capitalism, immature and weak, swung between two kinds of crisis. When choked in its growth by foreign capital, it had to make common cause with Chinese labor; but if the foreign grip eased a little, self-interest urged Chinese capital to pause in the long struggle for full independence and improve its own position at the expense of Chinese labor. For this and kindred reasons, dividing not only groups of Chinese from other groups but regions from other regions, the course of the Chinese Revolution as a whole veered first in one direction, then in another. From the foreign point of view, the variations were between "extremism," forcing foreign interests to make immediate concessions, and "moderation," allowing breathing spaces in which future concessions, hedged about with "ifs" and "buts," could be cautiously discussed.

These variations are reflected in the history of the Kuomintang or Nationalist Party which Sun Yat-sen formed out of a number of earlier revolutionary groups. Foreign governments, influenced by the "experts" of the time who believed in the "unchanging East" and the "lack of interest in politics of the ordinary Chinese," came to the support of the "moderate" faction composed of Chinese who had held high military and administrative positions under Manchu rule. To most of them the word "republic meant little more than the removal of the emperor and a chance to increase their own power. To some of them it meant merely an intermediate stage, leading up to the establishment of a new imperial government, under a Chinese emperor. The foreign governments were inclined to expect that the most powerful contemporary war lord, Yuan Shih-kai, who became first President of the Republic, would make himself emperor; and they were inclined to approve of such a step.

In this situation Sun Yat-sen remained a tenacious extremist. He wanted a republic in which there would be real processes of democratic, representative government. He perceived that the collective mind of China was really changing, even though the details of the democratic process of government under a republic were not yet widely understood. He was convinced that a Chinese emperor could only be installed with foreign support so strong that it would amount to control. He was supported by many wealthy businessmen who saw that a republic not established on a broad, democratic base still invited foreign interference and pressure which would strangle the expansion of independent Chinese business.

Sun Yat-sen knew China could only be saved by a multiple process. Penetration into China of European and American thought had to be encouraged but the penetration of European and American control had to be pushed back. The war lords who dominated the period from 1911 to 1926 also had to be overthrown, because they were only landlords writ large and armed with modern weapons. The businessmen alone could not overthrow them; nor could they flourish under them. Therefore the peasants had to be called in, as well as the labor groups. The movement was thus enlarged into one of the great revolutionary movements of history, uniting interests and schools of thought ranging from millionaires to Communists; but it went forward raggedly because businessmen, peasants, and labor did not want exactly the same things and did not want to move forward at the same speed.

Into this complicated situation there intruded the

influence of the Russian Revolution, the effects of which were felt all over Asia. We in America have never yet properly grasped the character of that influence. Wherever we see Russian influence, we still tend to look for Russian "agitators" upsetting the minds of people who would not make trouble if they were not "stirred up by troublemakers." We cannot understand either the Asia of yesterday or the Asia of today and tomorrow if we resort to such absurd simplifications. We must take the situation itself into account. All of the peoples of Asia, each in its degree – the subject colonial peoples and the people of China, whose liberty had been encroached on though not destroyed by nineteenth-century imperialism – were startled into hope, expectation, or political daydreaming by the Russian Revolution. Different peoples, and different groups within peoples, responded in different ways. There was a wide spread of response between those who merely hoped for a miracle and those who saw an opportunity for action.

The central fact, however, was a massive, roughhewn monument in history. A terrible war had just been fought. Rivalry over colonial possessions was one of the important causes of the war. Both Britain and France had brought colonial troops to fight in the decisive battles in Europe. As the fighting approached and reached its climax there had been talk of a war "to make the world safe for democracy," and of the self-determination of peoples; yet both

Britain and France had come out of the war with valuable additional colonial acquisitions, as mandatories of former enemy possessions. In the climate of Asia's thought – a jungle climate of illiteracy, of news and ideas transmitted by the spoken word, like legends and tales of wonder – the big and simple ideas had the best chance of survival. One tremendously potent idea was that freedom, the Wilsonian "self-determination," had been promised and then withheld. And in the minds of simple people, freedom was as much negative as positive; freedom not to be ruled by masters, sahibs, a race of alien lords from over the sea. Another idea, calling back hope when hope seemed gone, was that the masters had fallen out among themselves. One of the most powerful, brutal, and insensitive of the master peoples, the Russians, had overthrown its own masters, had summoned all other peoples to do the same, and was now held at bay by the remaining master peoples.

In this opposition of big, simple ideas the peoples of Asia either saw or hoped that they saw a community of interest between themselves and the Russians. They wanted to escape from colonial subjection. They wished the Russians well because the nations which were hostile to the emancipation of colonies were also hostile to Russia. Some hoped that they could somehow link up with the Russians in common action; others, of course, hoped for freedom without action, the gift of some strange but perhaps possible Russian miracle. This was a situation created only in part by the Russians. It was a situation, however, within which the Russian agents of the time worked very effectively, but they did so because the unrest on which they worked was already there; it was not an unrest which would not have existed but for "Bolshevik agitators."

China in the turbulent 1920's was the main focus of revolutionary activity in Asia; but the field as a whole was much wider than this focal area. As far west as Turkey the rise of Kemal put an end to a system similar to extraterritoriality in China. The Arab countries maneuvered to decrease their dependence on British and French tutelage. There were nationalist movements, with radical fringes, in Iran and Afghanistan. Unrest in India was only "kept in hand," to use one of the standard euphemisms, by measures ranging from the severe to the savage. An organized Burmese nationalism began to appear. Under the paternal autocracy of British rule in Malaya a small "modernist" group of Malays began to think and talk about democracy, and there was a more important political stirring among the Chinese and Indians in Malaya, related to movements in the home countries.

Even in Netherlands India, where the Dutch have carefully fostered a reputation for benevolent rule, there was vehement nationalism culminating in 1927 in an insurrection, put down with unhesitating cruelty, in which Communists were involved. An American author extremely sympathetic to official Dutch views records the deportation to New Guinea of "over a thousand communists, accompanied by their families." It seems reasonable to suppose that many of these were in fact nationalists rather than Communists, since the same author states that "what took place can probably best be explained as either communism using nationalism, or nationalism using communism for its own purposes."[1]

In Thailand there was no nationalist revolution until 1932 — perhaps because, making good use of Anglo-French rivalries, the Thais managed to negotiate, step by step, an evolution out of semicolonial control under treaties giving economic and political privileges to foreigners.

In Indo-China there was a Nationalist Party which resorted to terrorism, and a quite separate Communist Party founded about 1925 or 1926. A mutiny among native troops gave the French authorities an opportunity to resort to very brutal measures in repressing all political activity.

In Korea there was an appeal to the Versailles Conference, expressing with dramatic courage the demands for independence of an unarmed people. Peaceful demonstrations were broken up by the Japanese, and a vindictive terror followed against

[1] Amry Vandenbosch, *The Dutch East Indies*, 2nd ed., revised. University of California Press, p. 320.

all Koreans who had expressed even the mildest political ideas.

In the Philippines there was a steady widening of the franchise, and a steady growth in the prestige of Quezon and Osmeña. Progress toward independence met the terms formulated by Filipino leaders, even though there was danger that the independence aimed at would be weakened by economic hardship. Yet in the Philippines too there was some slight Communist activity, a mark of the resentment against imperialism prevailing all over Asia between world wars.[2]

In China the Second Revolution of 1925–1927 was able to take place at this time of general unrest because the international system of indirect control under treaty sanctions was cumbrous as compared with direct national control in colonial possessions. Even terroristic action, like firing on unarmed Chinese cities under the "gunboat policy," which permitted foreign warships to operate in Chinese territorial waters, could be resorted to only sporadically; it was not linked up with the kind of continuous, administrative police control which prevailed in the colonies.

[2] For a good survey of the period here summarized so briefly, see the study of "Nationalism and Nationalist Movements in Southeast Asia" by Virginia Thompson in *Government and Nationalism in Southeast Asia*, by Rupert Emerson, Lennox A. Mills, and Virginia Thompson. New York, 1942.

China was also a country in which right wing and left wing could work in alliance at that time. China's banks and the textile mills in which the first Chinese industrial capital was invested had grown rapidly during the European war but were still financially weak compared with the British, American, and Japanese banks in the Treaty Ports and the textile mills operated in China by the British and Japanese. Production, stimulated by the war, began after the war to shrink all over the world. The foreign interests in China saw no reason why the new Chinese enterprises should not be squeezed out by the shrinkage, leaving foreign enterprise as dominant as ever. Chinese capital, fighting for its life against foreign capital, was ready for an alliance with Chinese labor, and with the peasants too. Labor and the peasants, extremely weak in organization and immature even in political sophistication, could not think of challenging the middle classes in leadership, but were ready to form an enthusiastic following in a struggle for increased national independence.

China, struggling to throw off the economic control of the great capitalist countries, had a natural community of interest with Russia, politically and economically blockaded by the same countries. In China, the policy of the powers was to prevent a revolution which was trying to take place. In Russia, it was to defeat a revolution which had already taken place. Russia responded by making an agreement with Sun Yat-sen, declaring that the Soviet Union was in favor of the attainment of full independence and equality by China. The Russians eventually made available to China considerable numbers of personnel which must also have involved considerable expenditure and unknown but probably not very large quantities of supplies. No *quid pro quo* was demanded from the Chinese.

With the advantage of hindsight we can see that the Russian policy was reasonable and realistic, since the powers which were trying to hamstring the Chinese Revolution were also the powers which were trying to wreck the Russian Revolution. Any success of the Chinese was therefore in fact a *quid pro quo* in return for Russian aid. This, however, was not the way it looked to Europeans and Americans at the time. To them it looked like an attempt to expand the Russian Revolution into a world revolution; and this appeared to them to be confirmed by Sun Yat-sen's policy of admitting Communists to membership in the Kuomintang.

That was also the way it looked to some Russians. The majority policy of the Russian Communists was already oriented toward the defense and consolidation of what had already been won in Russia – the policy which was eventually to emerge and be defined as the Stalin policy of "socialism in one land." This policy, however, had not yet won the decision over the Trotsky policy of world revolution. The Trotsky faction was a very powerful minority within the Russian Communist Party, made still more powerful by its alliance with another minority led by Bukharin. The details of what went on in Russia at this time are still obscure and will remain obscure for a long time, but those who try to trace the course of the Chinese Revolution should always bear in mind the fact that open civil war in China was affected at every step by undeclared civil war in Russia.

There were Chinese Trotskyists and Bukharinists, just as there were Russian Trotskyists and Bukharinists. To some extent factions among the Chinese Communists were shadows of Russian factions, or of the factions which also were at odds with each other in the left-wing movements of Germany and the rest of Western Europe. In China, however, as in Russia, local problems were so urgent that they produced recognizable local interpretations of Marxist theory, out of which grew a distinct policy and leadership. The fact that Mao Tze-tung emerged from the radical movement within China and never studied abroad is to be compared with the fact that Stalin's character was formed in the underground movement in Russia, not in association with exiled revolutionaries abroad.

In 1927 the Kuomintang was a very wide coalition, which included the Communists among many other factions. Its military and political expansion from the deep south up to the Yangtze had been phenomenal. Peasant risings had facilitated the advance of the troops. Individual war lords, finding their troops going over to the revolutionaries, had been forced to join the Kuomintang themselves. Miners and factory workers ardently joined the revolution. Those Chinese capitalists whose interests were most competitive with foreign interests joined the movement of their own accord; those who were on the fence because their interests dovetailed with foreign interests were forced to join in order to save their enterprises. Revolutionary forces entered and took over the British Concession at Hankow, a Bastille of foreign vested interests in the heart of China. The International Settlement at Shanghai, the greatest Bastille of all, was in a state of siege. The factory workers, organized and to a certain extent armed, had opened the approaches to the Nationalist armies.

These developments brought on a crisis. How far would the foreigners give ground? Was the Chinese Revolution strong enough to face actual war against a foreign coalition? At Hankow the British had not fought; but at Wanhsien, also on the Yangtze, a British warship had answered rifle fire from the shore with naval gunfire against a crowded city, causing terrible slaughter. At Nanking, where several foreigners had been killed and most of the foreign community had gathered on a hilltop, American and British vessels laid down a barrage to enable them to evacuate. Shanghai, though threatened, was a foreign fortress with a strong garrison and a formidable concentration of warships.

This crisis was accompanied by a crisis within the revolutionary movement. As the coalition had grown wider, it had also become looser. There was less and less identity of conviction among those taking part. Those who had never wanted to be heroes, but had thought it better to go along, began to lag behind and to look for ways of slowing down the movement. Many of the late-joined militarists were also landlords, while the majority of their troops were peasants. Forced, as officers, to go along because otherwise their troops would have left them, they were worried, as landlords, by the thought of having to yield in a similar way to the demands of their peasants. Employers who had been glad to see their overstrong foreign competitors weakened by strikes did not want the movement to reach a point where Chinese workers became dominant over Chinese employers.

Out of this crisis a new coalition was formed, breaking up the old coalition. The new coalition, though narrower, was better able to concentrate its power. It was composed of those who thought that things had gone far enough, and that the time had come to consolidate the gains already made without risking defeat in an attempt to win more. It was dominated by bankers, industrialists, employers, landlords, and military leaders. The military leaders were an important element of fusion, because many of them had commercial connections or landlord interests, or both.

Those who were excluded from the coalition of compromise may be called, with some degree of oversimplification, the extremists. As time went on, "extremism" and "Communism" became more and more closely identified by the anti-Communists, but it is important to note that the original test of whether a man was an extremist or a compromiser was not whether he was Communist or anti-Communist, but whether or not he believed that the Chinese Revolution had won enough to make China safe. The original extremists included many besides the Communists who believed that compromise at the point reached in 1928 would leave foreign imperialism with so much power to interfere that it could continue to block the growth and development of China. Time was to prove that on this very important point those who were against compromise in 1928 were right. The privileges and controls which were still retained by the Treaty Powers after 1928 were used by Japan to deadly advantage in each step of aggression from 1931 to 1937.

Foreign interests in China also had their extremists and their compromisers. The extremists were the die-hards who believed that there would never be peace and security in the Far East until the Chinese were "taught a lesson"; and that the lesson ought to be military. As time went on, these die-hards tended to line up more and more openly with the Japanese. They were loud in justifying the Japanese invasion of Manchuria in 1931 and the savage Japanese attack on Shanghai in 1932. They continued to find excuses for Japan even in 1937 and later. Many of them were British, but some were American, and they had considerable influence with their governments. On the whole, however, the compromisers prevailed among the foreigners as they did among the Chinese. The British must be given the credit for leading the way, with the rendition of several minor concessions in addition to the Hankow concession; and there followed a number of financial and tariff policies which increased the revenue of the Chinese Government and the ability of Chinese enterprise to compete with foreign enterprise.

The Chinese National Government which continues in power to this day was made possible by the fact that both Chinese and foreigners were willing to compromise in 1928. It enjoyed more foreign economic and financial co-operation than any previous Chinese Government. It is essential to our understanding of contemporary China to remember this foreign strand woven into the fabric of the Chinese National Government. It is essential also to remember something which was not appreciated soon enough by most foreigners, either businessmen or political analysts: community of interest between foreign enterprise – principally

British and American – and the Chinese Government made Japan from 1928 onward as much the enemy of Britain and America as it was the enemy of China.

From the moment the new Chinese coalition was formed, Chiang Kai-shek became its personal focus and symbol. The nature of the coalition which he headed explains why he has never been a dictator, though he has been called a dictator by his enemies and though some of his followers have experimented in reorganizing the Kuomintang on fascist lines.[3]

As the symbol of a new phase in China, Chiang had remarkable qualifications. He had been a

[3] Chiang had also to make use of foreign support without becoming a dictator on behalf of foreign interests, which in China have always groped toward the "strong man" solution of the problem of law and order. In a country as weakly organized as China, where foreign interests are strongly organized, they feel most nearly at ease when they can present their demands to some one man. When they can find such a man – a Li Hung-chang at the end of the nineteenth century, a Yuan Shih-kai at the beginning of the twentieth century – they are always willing to give him enough support in loans, military equipment, and training for his troops to make him strong enough to control the country on their behalf. Chiang Kai-shek lifted himself and his country above this level, and has always been supported by the middle classes because he has represented them in their long struggle to become independent, not only of foreign countries but of foreign interests.

favorite disciple of Sun Yat-sen and could thus claim a direct political heritage. His family came from that upper stratum of the farming class which is familiar with the outlook both of the landlord and of the tenant, and with business transactions as they are carried on by village merchants and moneylenders. Prosperous peasants of this kind, if they are unlucky or not thrifty, can easily lose their own land and become tenants; if they are frugal and industrious, they can often become small landlords. It is common for them to own land and work it themselves, and also to rent extra land and farm it either through a subtenant or through hired labor. An observant man of this class is excellently placed to know the mind and pulse of rural China.

Chiang was educated at Paotingfu, in the first modern academy in China for professional officers. Men from this academy were usually nationalist and patriotic in their outlook, even though they had to serve perforce in various war-lord armies. Through them Chiang had a fellow-cadet relationship with the best professional soldiers in China. Later he studied in Japan, widening both his military and his political contacts. Americans usually overlook the important fact that Chinese who have studied in Japan are much more numerous than those who have studied in America, are equally influential in politics, administration, and business, and much more influential in the army. In China, with its revolutionary problems, the soldier must necessarily have a political mind. The American Army knows fewer of the political facts of life than any army in the world. Chinese graduates of West Point and Virginia Military Institute have therefore rarely got anywhere in China. The Japanese Army, on the other hand, is imbued with politics; and Chinese officers who have studied in Japan form powerful cliques both in the national and provincial armies and in the politics of China.

For an interval in his life, Chiang was a broker and businessman in Shanghai. He thus came in touch with the young generation of Chinese finance and industry, and learned to know both its foreign affiliations and its foreign antagonisms. Shanghai, moreover, like Chicago, was a city in which business was politics, politics was business, and gangsterism was both big business and big politics. Shanghai's gangsters were in part a new, big-city development of old secret societies with political traditions. They were an obvious source of recruitment for the secret police which are indispensable to a young government founded by a revolutionary movement.

Chiang was also one of the non-Communist members of the Kuomintang whom Sun Yat-sen sent to Russia in 1923 to study political and military organization. On his return he took charge of the Whampoa Military Academy at which were trained the officers of the new revolutionary elite who led the armies that marched to the Yangtze and beyond. The old Paotingfu professionals and the Whampoa elite have strongly distinct group loyalties and Chiang is one of the few who have a high standing in both groups. Chiang's Russian experience was important when the Kuomintang dismissed its Russian advisors and split with the Chinese Communists; his position was not that of an ignorant anti-Russian, but that of a man who had studied Communist organization and Russian methods in the Soviet Union.

Finally, by his marriage with the present Madame Chiang, the Generalissimo, whose experience outside of China did not include either America or Western Europe, became associated with one of the most able and influential American-educated families in China. Its contacts included business groups, missionary groups, and Chinese Christian groups, and through these contacts Chiang could draw freely on the able personnel of the American-educated Chinese.

Every one of these influences which formed part of the personal experience of Chiang Kai-shek the individual was reflected also in the coalition which controlled the Kuomintang after 1928. No two or three of the elements involved could have formed a subcoalition without throwing out of balance the coalition as a whole. The problem of statesmanship was therefore the maintenance of poise.

In spite of the power he held through control of this coalition, Chiang never became a dictator or a fascist. Accusations of dictatorship and fascism have obscured his real claim to be a coalition statesman of genius. True fascism is created when a very narrow coalition of big business and big militarism decides to set up a dictator who will be the master of the nation but the servant of the inside ring. A dictator has to have real power in order to put himself across, and therefore his backers have to have real power to delegate to him. In China this was impossible because neither business nor militarism had a decisive margin of real power to give away.

The second stage in the growth of a fascist dictatorship is when the dictator turns on his controllers, using the power which they delegated to him to bring them under control. In the case of both the personal fascism of Mussolini and Hitler and the group fascism of Japan, this stage was never actually completed, but got only to the point of an uneasy partnership between the dictatorship and its backers, alternately cordial and hostile. This never quite completed decision, entailing a search for enough compensation to satisfy all the partners, provided a powerful head of steam behind the fascist drive of aggression abroad. In all mature fascist structures, however, there did emerge one clear mark of the power of the dictator: his ability to make his orders carry all the way down through the lower ranks.

By this very important test, Chiang Kai-shek must clearly be described as an arbiter, not a dictator. Although his personal power increased very greatly after 1928, his ability to make decisions continued to depend on a process by which big and little questions, of an enormous variety, were passed up to him from below. Because of the variety of the component elements of the coalition over which he presided, each deadlock between interested groups meant an appeal that had to be passed up to him for decision. It is for this reason that Chinese widely admire in Chiang something which few Westerners have appreciated: his ability to give decisions which break deadlocks, but do not upset the balance of the component elements within the Kuomintang coalition. It took the long war with Japan to destroy that balance, as will be seen in the next chapter.

CHAPTER IV

CHINA'S PARTY POLITICS AND THE WAR WITH JAPAN

ONE of Chiang Kai-shek's most solid claims to a place in history is that he personally was responsible for the decision to risk China's very existence as a nation in a final stand against Japan, and for the timing of that decision. The still inadequately organized China which he had at his back when he took the decision and made the stand was, however, in part the creation of American and British policy. The importance of this fact has never been realized, much less admitted, by American public opinion.

There can be no doubt that when the foreigners, both businessmen and diplomats, came to terms with the government controlled by Chiang Kai-shek, they thought they had found the man they wanted to rule China in their interest. Nor can there be any doubt that Chiang saw what the game was and knew that the dice were loaded, but still thought that he could play the game and win — and he did win. The civil war against the Chinese Communists from 1928 to the end of 1936 became the symbol of the fact that the game was being played. In fact the score of the game, throw by throw, can be traced through the stages of this bitter war.

Through civil war against the Communists Chiang was able to regulate the interests of the varied groups within the Kuomintang coalition. In effect, he could say to any of these groups when he was called on to adjust their differences, "You must accept my solution, otherwise the Communist situation will get out of hand, and that will be worse for you than what I now propose." In the same way, the civil war could be used to improve his bargaining position in negotiations with foreign powers. In effect, he could say to them, "You must concede me the minimum that I ask in negotiating credits, tariff revisions, the gradual adjustment of the old unequal treaties in China's favor, because otherwise people will begin to go over to the Communists, whose demands are much more extreme than mine." Even in evading and fencing with the Japanese the same kind of argument could be used. As a screen for their increasing aggression, the Japanese claimed to be "the bulwark against Bolshevism in Asia." Chiang's riposte was to show that he was the bulwark against Bolshevism in China.

Finally, the war against the Communists was used to build up a national army in the face of the conventional thinking of the imperial powers who favored a Chinese army of a colonial type – one that would enable Chiang to crush peasant rebellions and keep provincial war lords in line, but not one that would enable him to face an invading army on equal terms. It was easy and profitable to unload obsolete tanks, second-line planes, and all kinds of surplus equipment on China. It was not to the interest of the Japanese militarists, however, even to allow all the provincial militarists to be subordinated to the national government. It was their set policy to oppose unity in China, and they therefore sold arms both to Chiang Kai-shek's government and to war lords who opposed Chiang Kai-shek.

In spite of all difficulties, however, Chiang succeeded in building up an army not only good enough to give him superiority in civil war, but good enough to face an invasion. In this he was helped by his German advisors, who were influenced by conflicting and very interesting motives. Germany, after Hitler came to power in 1933, was committed to a community of interest with Japan, though not to an identity of interest. Even before Hitler, however, the Reichswehr had decided that in preparation for the next war it could profit from the study of any kind of war, under any conditions of terrain or politics. German officers did not go to China casually, in search of adventure or good pay. They were selected by the General Staff for their intelligence and ability, and their mission was as much to learn as to teach. In training troops to fight the Communists they studied the use of regular troops against partisans, and also the ways in which troops with inferior equipment can by skill in maneuver and use of terrain maintain fronts against superior forces. It is beyond question that they learned a great deal in China, and it is not to be doubted that they discussed with the Chinese Staff the problems of resisting a Japanese invasion, in which the ratio of inferiority of the Chinese regular army to the Japanese would be comparable to the ratio of inferiority of the Chinese Communists to the Chinese regulars.

It is a bad blot on the record of American and British officers that they did not study the same problems with the same realism – with a few still unappreciated exceptions like Colonel Carlson of the Marines – and consequently misjudged the whole nature of the Japanese war in China as badly as they later misjudged the German invasion of Russia. We have printed proof of how much the Germans learned in China, which is worth a digression here because it is also an indication that the Reichswehr knew why it disagreed with Hitler's strategy in Russia.

In July 1938, a young German correspondent in China who was in close touch with the German Military Mission wrote an article on "Space as a Weapon" in the Chinese-Japanese war. The Germans were just then being withdrawn from China as a concession to Hitler's friendship with Japan. The article, dated July, was published in General

Haushofer's extremely influential *Zeitschrift für Geopolitik* for September 1938 – a month before the fall of Hankow and Canton. Among the points which it made were the following: –

1. Japan, trying to cut up China piecemeal, misunderstood the factor of China's great depth of terrain and failed to cope with it properly, which "is interesting . . . because similar conditions exist elsewhere in the world" – a hint at the nature of war in Russia.

2. China is described as "believe it or not . . . stronger than at the beginning of the war."

3. Writing several months before the fall of Hankow, the author predicted that it would fall and that this would in effect leave two separate territories of Free China, one in the northwest and one in the southwest.

4. "It is obvious that after the capture of Hankow the Chinese Army will be driven back but not annihilated."

5. "If the Japanese wished to start a policy of swift annihilation now they would have to realize that it is too late . . . China's area ensures its survival and for that reason it would be best for the Japanese to make peace."[1]

Apart from the interest of the article as a fore-

[1] Wolf Schenke, "Raum als Waffe," *Zeitschrift für Geopolitik*, Sept. 1938. Quotations are from the translation published in *Amerasia*, New York, Jan. 1939, under the title "Vast Area as an Instrument of War."

sighted and accurate analysis of the war theater in China, it seems that it must have been published as a discreet, indirect Reichswehr warning to Hitler not to invade Russia, since there could be no joint action with a Japan which had already overreached itself in China. The whole tenor of the article contrasts instructively with the opinion of America's leading foreign commentator that by taking Canton the Japanese had "won the war." (See page 11.)

To return to the course of civil war in China. There were several phases of this war and its accompanying political developments, shading in and out of each other in a way that is difficult to describe without making the transitions appear sharper than they really were. The first phase was one of extremism. Although many besides the Communists had their doubts in 1928 whether the time had really come for a right-wing compromise within the Kuomintang, and a compromise between the Chinese Revolution and the foreign interests whose controls it was attempting to throw off, only the hardest-minded men were willing to carry their opposition to the length of civil war.

From the beginning the extremists were dominated by the Communists. The great majority of the professional officers went with the Kuomintang and Chiang Kai-shek. As was to be expected, the troops who stood by them were the most professional troops, those who had been longest under discipline and had the best equipment. Most of the war-lord troops, whose morale was of a half-feudal kind, colored by personal allegiance to the war lord who paid them, were also against the Communists. This left the Communists with a military nucleus of men who were either armed industrial workers or peasants who had a high revolutionary morale but comparatively little training as professional soldiers.

One wing of the Communists believed in revolutionary ardor and the offensive at all costs. The leaders who tried to make this the "party line" threw away their best troops in trying to take cities and important strategic centers. The leadership then passed to Mao Tze-tung and Chu Teh, the men who have since become the legendary figures of Chinese Communism. These men foresaw a long struggle against superior forces with better equipment. They needed time to train their men in the kind of war they foresaw, and they believed it imperative to get behind them a solid civilian support. Under Chinese conditions this meant that they had to retire to an area of undeveloped communications and few large cities and base themselves on the support of poor peasants. These conditions explain the savagery and slaughter of the first period of Kuomintang-Communist war.

The Communists have now won a relatively favorable place in American public opinion, but questions are still sometimes asked about this earlier period. The answer is that the Kuomintang was out to crush the Communists before they could rally and consolidate. The Communists could not survive unless they got food, shelter, guides to show them the terrain, and information about the movements of the enemy. They could not win over the peasants by giving lectures on Marxism. They had to do things which would utterly and irrevocably commit them to the peasant cause and make it clear that they were not war-lord troops who would sell out.

There was only one thing to do: take land from the landlords, give it to the peasants, and then join with the peasants in defending the land against both the landlords and the Kuomintang's armies. Many large landlords of the more feudal kind, in backward parts of China, have their own armed retainers. Often these landlords resisted expropriation. They were killed – there being no time to persuade them – in a Red Terror. Later, as the fight for survival became desperate and bitter, the Red Terror turned not only against those who resisted, but against anyone whose loyalty was in doubt. Both sides, in fact, fought a merciless, Old Testament, Hebrew-and-Philistine war, applying ruthlessly the test that "he who is not with us is against us."

The White Terror, it should be pointed out, was as bad as the Red in the things done, and worse in the number of people to whom things were done. For every landlord or "bourgeois" killed, scores of peasants were slaughtered, tortured, or burned in their villages; untold numbers of peasant girls were sold into brothels and boys into bondage. In China, as in Pilsudski's Poland, in the Baltic States, and in Mannerheim's Finland, the White Terror was worse than the Red because in a peasant country revolution attempts to break the grip of a minority, while counterrevolution attempts to break the will of a majority.

Among the Communists in this period the processes of coalition were unimportant. The vast majority were peasants. There were intellectuals and urban proletarian workers among the leaders, but these were people who had been torn from their origins and local contacts. There was no question of compromise between the Communists and foreign interests, if only for the reason that the Communists were geographically not in contact with foreign interests. Even more important is the fact that the Chinese Communists were so isolated, south of the Yangtze and far inland from the coast, that they could not receive arms or any other help from Russia, while the intensity of the fight for survival made it impossible for them to slacken or strengthen their civil-war efforts in accordance with "directives" from either the Third International or the Soviet Government. They were on their own.

A second phase of the civil war can be dated approximately from the Japanese invasion of Manchuria in 1931. The shock of this invasion was important in two ways. First it tended to support the opinion of those, including many who had not gone along with the Communists, who had all along contended that China in 1926–1927 had not loosened the foreign grip enough to make herself safe. Second, it followed a peaceful agreement by which the Northeastern Provinces (Manchuria) had submitted to the National Government without civil war – an omen that it was not yet safe for China to consolidate in peace without being prepared to defend her consolidations against foreign attack.

Five months later, in February 1932, the Chinese Communists "declared war" against the Japanese – a declaration which has to be cited in quotation marks, because there was no way in which the Communists could get at the Japanese to fight them. At the same time the Communists issued an appeal for a United Front. In 1933 this appeal was followed up by an offer to co-operate with any Kuomintang army against the Japanese; but the government ignored the appeal and kept up the civil war relentlessly, forcing the Communists to begin, in 1934, their famous Long March from south of the Yangtze westward to the edges of Tibet and then northward and northeastward to the Yellow River province of Shensi, in the northern part of which they consolidated themselves in 1935 and 1936. Mao Tze-tung confessed to Edgar Snow that this move was partly made necessary by losses suffered in a mistaken attempt to fight the Kuomintang armies in positional warfare; but he claimed also to have made the move partly in order to get into a better position to deal with the situation arising out of Japanese aggression.[2]

There were two main characteristics of this second phase. On the one hand the Communists, though still not in a position to convert themselves into a coalition party, began to acquire a significant number of sympathizers within the much greater territory controlled by the Kuomintang, because of their demand for an end to civil war and a united stand against the Japanese. On the other hand, events outside of the Kuomintang-Communist civil war were forcing a final crisis between China and Japan.

1. The Germans and Italians in Europe, and the Japanese in Asia, were working a seesaw – but against whom? The most influential American and European experts held that it was against Russia, or could be turned against Russia. Actually, the indications are that the Rome-Berlin-Tokyo Axis had decided, long before the appeasement powers were aware of it, to leave Russia alone for the time being and attack the appeasement powers first. In view of our policy in Spain, our attitude toward Hitler at the time of Munich and after Munich, and

[2] The statements in this paragraph are based on Edgar Snow, *Red Star Over China*, Random House, Inc., New York, 1938, p. 166.

our Asiatic policy of protest without resistance, America must be included with the appeasement powers.

One indication of German policy has already been quoted. In 1937, a few weeks before the Marco Polo Bridge incident which opened the all-out war in China, there was an even more revealing indication of Japan's higher strategy. A flare-up of hostilities along the Amur River frontier between Manchuria and Siberia led to wide speculation. When the Japanese, instead of going ahead with the invasion of Siberia, turned suddenly against China, the conclusion of the most influential experts was that the Japanese had tested the Russians and found that they were not to be feared. It is much more probable that the Japanese tested the Russians, found that they were strong and, even more important, that they would fight at the drop of the hat and keep on fighting, and therefore resigned themselves to an invasion of China without first pinching off Vladivostok and securing their rear.

2. In China all through the year 1936 the Japanese hoped that Chiang Kai-shek could be bluffed into letting them occupy a big and strategically vital territory between the Great Wall and the Yellow River. The coalition headed by Chiang was known to be badly split. Wang Ching-wei, who later went over to the Japanese, held at that time the position equivalent to Premier in the Chinese Government,

and was known to be defeatist. Many of China's industrialists and bankers were known to be for peace at any price, because their main wealth was in factories, machines, and warehouses in the port cities, defenseless against the Japanese Navy.

3. If the Chinese were to resist, there was the further question of timing the call to the nation to resist. Chiang had faced the ultimate necessity for resistance as early as 1931–1932, and had worked steadily to prepare for the war, knowing that he would at first get only wobbly "moral support" from America and Britain, but believing that in the end Japanese encroachment on American and British interests would force more positive aid. The only question was one of timing. Chiang held on until the last possible moment in the hope that he would be able to break the military power of the Communists before he had to face the military power of Japan.

In holding to this line he was supported, or at least not restrained, by American and British policy. In view of the fact that our present policy openly encourages a negotiated settlement between Kuomintang and Communists, and deplores the possibility of civil war, it is important to recall that in all the published American official documents covering policy in the years between the invasion of Manchuria in 1931 and the invasion of the main body of China in 1937, there is not a hint that we ever urged a negotiated national unity in China. In my opinion this forces us to draw a very sobering inference: The unity of China was not a prime requisite because in Washington and London too we were at this time either fumbling instinctively or working calculatedly toward a "settlement" which would allow Japan actual gains at the expense of China, while impairing as little as possible the legal purity and financial value of our own rights and privileges.

During this period the Communists pressed and propagandized for a negotiated end to the civil war and a full stand against Japan at the earliest possible moment rather than the last possible moment. By so doing they invested themselves with a new political character. They ceased to be merely a party which *opposed* the policy of the government and became a party with a policy *alternative* to that of the government. Furthermore, although they remained a one-doctrine party and could not yet broaden out into a coalition, they became potentially the focus of a new coalition because a number of movements outside of Communist territory, and not in the least Communist in character, began to urge the National Government to accede to the policy advocated by the Communists.

At Christmas time in 1936 the electric question of sooner or later was decided. With this decision the civil-war phase of China's internal politics passed into a new phase of war for national survival. Some of the troops lined up against the Communists in Northwest China had become impatient of civil war and eager to fight Japan instead, and had even begun to fraternize with the Communists. At a time when probably not one of the generals under him would have had the courage to do so, Chiang Kai-shek went personally to the center of disaffection to restore discipline, and was kidnaped by the mutineers. There were three immediate reactions to the kidnaping. There were popular demonstrations all over the country – spontaneous and not drummed up by political organizers – hailing Chiang Kai-shek as the national leader and representative of the whole people, and demanding that he be released immediately. The Communists themselves joined in this demand for unconditional release, sending a representative to the center of the mutiny to take part in negotiations. On the other hand, some of the more rigidly military minds in the National Government wanted to send a punitive expedition against the mutineers, regardless of whether this might cost the Generalissimo his life.

Madame Chiang Kai-shek and her brother T. V. Soong, without the protection of a strong bodyguard, both flew to Sian. The Generalissimo himself took a line of the severest dignity and courage, refusing to discuss any conditions whatever and insisting on the duty of the mutineers to submit to their commander in chief. He won. It was the greatest victory of his life, and it united China. Although no bargain had been struck, the way was now open for a negotiated United Front between the Kuomintang and its only armed opponents, the Communists, and consequently for a united stand against the Japanese.

If it was plain to the Chinese that they could now unite, it was plain to the Japanese that they had to strike before the new unity could solidify. They struck at the Marco Polo Bridge, six months later, on July 7, 1937. They failed to engineer a limited war, and found themselves swept into the unlimited war which is still going on. The changes that have taken place during the war are of great importance, and it is necessary to know what has happened if we are to understand the political fabric of China today and the trend of possibility or probability for the future.

From the outbreak of war in 1937 to the fall of Canton and Hankow, in October 1938, China showed a political cohesion that astonished foreign observers. By taking Shanghai, the Japanese themselves prevented any important appeasement by wealthy Chinese who, under the influence of the conservatism that goes with property, might have tried to come to terms with them. At the same time all Chinese were inspired by the stubborn defense of Shanghai, which proved once for all that the Japanese were no supermen, even when relative superiority of naval guns, planes, tanks, and artillery ought to have made them supermen. The Chinese were also buoyed up by the conviction that by forcing the Japanese out of a "limited war" in North China into a general war all over China, and by completely upsetting the Japanese timetable, they had by their own will and courage imposed a long war on the Japanese instead of a blitzkrieg. Since this was a defeat of Japan's master strategy, it held out hopes for eventual Chinese victory. In this period there was remarkably good co-ordination between the Communist troops and the national armies, considering that the United Front had been formed only at the last minute and considering the distrust and enmity accumulated during ten years of civil war. There was also a heartening fervor in the spread of guerilla war behind the Japanese lines.

There was a change, radical in nature though gradual in development, after the fall of Hankow and Canton, which divided China into a Northwestern area and a Southwestern area, not too efficiently joined together (because of transport difficulties) by the province of Szechwan, in which stands Chungking, the wartime capital.

In this situation China began to fight a stalemate war, in the strategy of which there was an important assumption: that Japanese failure to win a decision would generate pressures forcing Japan to encroach on the interests of other nations and forcing these nations to line up definitely with China. This assumption is stated, carefully but with less circumlocution than is usual in diplomatic language, in a "message to friendly Powers" from Chiang

Kai-shek on the second anniversary of the war, July 7, 1939. It was broadcast to America in translation by Madame Chiang: –

> Japan's invasion of China now enters its third year and becomes more vicious every day. It now assumes the added form of an anti-foreign movement calculated to drive all Occidental rights and interests from Asia. The Powers, if only in defense of their own rights, should take more positive action. China is determined to carry on her resistance indefinitely. She will not disappoint her many friends who have given her so generously both moral and material assistance.
>
> The nations of the world are now so interdependent that China cannot get along without the co-operation of the West, and the West cannot get along without China. . . . In a word, we must do everything possible to frustrate the Japanese plan of establishing a "New Order in East Asia," which, in its final analysis, means Japanese domination of Asia and the closing of the "Open Door" to the West.[3]

The assumption was correct, as Pearl Harbor proved; but there was one doubtful factor, the factor of time. If Japan had moved against the Western powers earlier, the approaches to China might still have been kept open, and relief from the West might have come in such a form and at such

[3] *Resistance and Reconstruction. Messages During China's Six Years of War, 1937–1943.* By Generalissimo Chiang Kai-shek. New York, 1943.

a time that the National Government would have emerged with a clear ascendancy over the Communists. The fact that the Japanese delayed the attack on Pearl Harbor until the very end of 1941 gave time for a full development of the differences between government policy and Communist policy. In addition, the differences between the two policies were emphasized by the isolation of China when the Philippines, Hong Kong, Singapore, and Burma fell so rapidly, cutting China off from supplies in quantity, while simultaneously Russia was extended to the utmost in checking the huge weight of the German assault.

During this period the Kuomintang underwent a transformation, largely invisible and therefore little noticed by conventional experts. Of the coalition composing the Kuomintang, the bankers and industrialists, by being driven into the far interior, had lost most of the tangible property and the structure of trading connections on which their power and political influence were based. Consequently, there began a subtle change in the relations between them and the Kuomintang Party functionaries and government administrators. Once their opinions and wishes had had great influence on party decisions and government policies. Now, it was they who had to defer to bureaucrats and functionaries. The pitifully small percentage of machinery which had been salvaged from the industrial cities could not be set up again without consulting officials who knew the government's war plans. Even more important, the government, because of the terrible dislocation of the whole country's financial structure, became rapidly more important as the major source of both investment capital and working capital, provided through grants and subsidies. Government functionaries, in a word, became members of boards of directors, while former managing directors and members of boards became subsidiary business bureaucrats.

Increase of bureaucratic authority in an agrarian society is incapable of mobilizing a war economy efficiently. The increase in the number of bureaucrats in Washington, though unpopular with businessmen, has been an essential part of our spectacular economic mobilization, because the men and women involved are members of an industrial society and a large proportion of them understand organization, know how to enforce it, and want to enforce it. In China a high proportion of the personnel of bureaucracy sympathize not with the need for efficiency but with those who demand special favors – which, in an agrarian society, means the influential landlords. As Sun Fo puts it, "Since the war, the tyrannous grip [of the corrupt gentry and rapacious landlords] has been tighter than ever. Taking advantage of the government measures for the collection of grain and the conscription of soldiers, these people have increased their power for evil-doing. . . ." [4]

Just before the war, the largest and most calculable single source of government revenue had been the customs duties collected on import and export trade. With the loss of the seaports, this revenue was abruptly cut down. Farm production now became the most important national source of revenue, in addition to being by far the most important economic activity in Free China – and all the more so because of the government's huge needs for feeding the armies, and because rice and grain can be stored and transported, and therefore, within a truncated economic system, serve as important media for the investment and transfer of surplus wealth.

The importance of the land tax collected either in money or in grain is an ancient tradition in China; but so is the difficulty of collecting it. The inadequacy of statistics is pathetic, and the confusion of land deeds and titles is fantastic. In some important areas, the last land survey was made in the sixteenth century. In every rural district the landlords, and the merchants and bailiffs whose interests are allied with theirs, are literate; the majority of the peasants are not. A large proportion of county magistrates and lesser officials, therefore, come from landlord families, and an overwhelming proportion have

[4] *China Looks Forward*, by Sun Fo. John Day Company, New York, 1944, p. 120.

interests or connections allied to those of the landlords. Consequently, it is simply impossible to collect the land tax without the good will of the landlords, and usually this good will boils down to a simple proposition: the landlord must be called in to help; he must be allowed to pass on his share of the tax to the peasants, in the form of increased rent, and if the government wishes to increase its revenues, the landlord must be allowed to increase his also.

The outcome is as simple as the explanation. The influence of landlords over party functionaries and government officials has grown greater at the same time that the influence of party functionaries and government officials over bankers and industrialists and businessmen has grown greater. Thus the Kuomintang, with few overt changes to mark the transition, has in fact largely ceased to function as a coalition party, and has become more and more a landlord party. Business interests have not been eliminated and they have not ceased to make money, but they have become subordinate where they were once dominant. Since they alone cannot offset the landlord interest, they need a widening of the coalition in order to regain their ascendancy, and they are therefore less implacably hostile to the groups led by the Communists than are the landlords.

While the Kuomintang was moving from a coalition of interests toward a monopoly of one interest, the Communists were moving in the opposite direction. From being a one-doctrine party, they were tending to become a coalition party. This trend was produced by imperative pressures. During the ten years of civil war the Communists, cut off from cities and urban workers, had become a peasant party. They had been able to survive only by winning to their support the largest possible number of peasants, no matter how bloody and merciless the war in which this policy involved them with the landlords. In a war against the Japanese, however, this policy would have meant annihilation, not survival. Japanese political warfare relied strongly on persuading the landlords that Japan would defend them against Bolshevism. It would have been fatal to drive a whole class of Chinese, and many of those dependent on them, into alliance with the Japanese.

The Communists therefore changed their policy. They ceased to expropriate land, unless the landlord went over to the Japanese. They left the landlord on his land, and they defended the land for him against the Japanese; but in return they drastically limited the amount of rent which he was allowed to collect from his tenants. The reduction of rent, in turn, was large enough to retain the allegiance of the peasants. A parallel policy was adopted in production and trade. With the big cities all in the hands of the Japanese, the Communists had nothing to fear from Chinese big business. With nothing to rely on but rural resources, they did need to fear economic paralysis. They therefore thought it to their interest to encourage and protect both private enterprise and co-operative enterprise, and to allow room for private profit as the quickest and surest stimulus for production and distribution.

Finally, having created nothing less than a new coalition of group interests, they took the logical step of allowing political expression for all groups within the coalition. Probably the most significant report brought back by the American newspapermen who visited the Communist area in the summer of 1944 was the confirmation of what was previously known only through Communist propaganda: actual operation of the Communist one-in-three system limiting Communist membership in committees and local governing bodies and the higher councils of the whole area to one third of the total membership. This is the most positive step yet taken in China by any party away from dictatorship and toward democracy. It confirms the graduation of the Communists from being a perpetual minority opposition party to the status of a party which has good claims to a position within a coalition government.

These comparisons of change and trend are important because of a factor whose importance is not discussed often enough in America. Up to 1944 the Japanese had occupied only about a third of China's territory; but that third was the home of about half of China's population — and the half which before 1937 contained by far the largest proportions of prosperous, educated, and politically sophisticated people. It is this part of China, including the Northeastern Provinces (Manchuria), which has actually experienced what Japanese rule means. It is in this part of China also that the chief contact between the people and their distant government in Chungking has been through propaganda. A major emphasis in that propaganda has been on the future democracy for which China is fighting.

When the Japanese are driven out, the political program of the forces which drive them out or follow them up will be of critical importance. If the actual policy put into practice is not one of free political organization and representation, or at the very least a coalition policy representing all major groups, there will be terrible disillusionment and political unrest. In view of all this it is realistic to allow for the fact that the Kuomintang has been weakened by the trend toward landlord domination during the war years, because the landlord interest will instinctively move toward control of the peasants, not toward allowing them political representation, when Occupied China is liberated from the Japanese. Conversely, the coalition trend of the Communists has put them in a strong position to make a bid for wider allegiances when, on the heels of the Japanese, their columns march parallel with those of the National Government into recovered territory.

CHAPTER V

WAR, PRESTIGE, AND POLITICS

THERE have been changes, during the war, in the prestige of every one of the countries now at war. In each case, the military factors of prestige have interacted with political factors.

China's prestige was at its highest from the end of 1938, when the loss of Hankow and Canton failed to break Chinese resistance, to the end of 1942 when it began to appear certain that so much of the work of defeating Japan would be done by America that China was in increasing danger of appearing at the peace table as a beneficiary rather than a full partner of victory. During the period of high Chinese prestige there was an unfortunate tendency in America toward undiscriminating praise of China, its government, and its armies. A great part of the total volume of praise contented itself with referring to China's continuing resistance as a "miracle." Accurate analysis of the factors of Chinese resistance did not have a wide general circulation. Now that China's prestige has markedly declined, criticism of the Chinese, their government, and their armies is equally undiscriminating. Extreme swings of the pendulum of American public opinion are dangerous. They make difficult the practice of a wise national policy. They encourage the obscurantism which is the occupational disease of diplomats, and which can only be checked by the steady pressure of an informed public opinion which knows what it wants, and why.

China's prestige was highest when the whole world could feel, though few people knew the details of Chinese politics, that the Chinese were determined to resist Japanese conquest, with or without aid from abroad. Had China's resistance not been of this kind, one nation after another would have come to terms with Japan in time to sell the Japanese militarists enough equipment to win the decisive victory which they were in fact unable to win without foreign complaisance. As long as the Chinese neither wavered nor split up, public opinion, confused though it was, would not allow "deals" at the expense of China, and the worst that the most appeasement-minded governments could do was to see that China got enough to keep up resistance, while allowing Japan enough to keep on attacking.

As a footnote to history, it is worth adding that perhaps there was one decisive difference between the brave Czechoslovaks, who only cracked when intolerable German pressure was backed by France and Britain, and not opposed by America, and the Chinese, who did not crack even when their country was invaded. The Czechoslovaks felt unable at the final crisis to call for Russian help in the face of the disapproval of the Western powers, while the Chinese Government, in spite of its cold hostility to Communism, realized that the acceptance of Russian supplies and even military advisors and aviators was effective in keeping up a minimum of American and British aid.

There was a setback to Chinese prestige late in 1940 and early in 1941 when Chinese unity was broken by tension between the New Fourth Army and the Chinese High Command, ending in an attack on the New Fourth by government troops. This clash was a symptom of the stalemate phase of war that had set in after the fall of Hankow and Canton, and the beginning of the landlord ascendancy in the Kuomintang, described in the previous chapter. The New Fourth was a half-regular, half-guerilla army. It was not a Communist army, but it contained Communist elements and its deputy commander was a Communist; the formation of such an army had been possible only under the conditions of enthusiastic unity in 1937 and 1938. Once the major fronts had begun to settle into a deadlock this army, which was linked with the Chinese front but also operated behind the Japanese lines, could remain active only if it relied more and more on organizing the peasants. War in this manner ran counter to the landlord interest because, if the deadlock were to end in a war between Japan and other countries, the landlords might return, after the eventual defeat of Japan, only to find that the peasants had become organized so strongly that landlord control could not be reasserted.

Chinese prestige rose again, however, after Pearl Harbor, though not at once. At first the ominous procession of defeats from Pearl Harbor to the Philippines, Singapore, the Netherlands Indies, and Burma induced a panicky fear in America and Britain that China might collapse. Undoubtedly this fear was linked psychologically with an old, complacent habit of thinking that America and Britain were superior nations and China an inferior nation. If the Japanese were strong enough to knock the lords of creation so cavalierly, how could China not collapse? Yet China did not collapse, and as a matter of fact it needed no mysterious inside knowledge to explain why China did not collapse. The Chinese were terribly disappointed by the first setbacks to their new allies; but they never for a moment doubted that these allies would recover. The major element of uncertainty in hanging on through several years of stalemate war had now settled in China's favor: China had allies. The time it might take for these allies to recover from their defeat and take the offensive was only a minor uncertainty. Not even the most conscienceless traitor would now sell out to Japan, because there is no point in selling out to a certain loser. Be that as it may, however, the fact that the Chinese did not collapse raised their prestige once more.

The more recent decline in Chinese prestige is related to a change in the character of the war in the Chinese theater, not to be confused with any supposed doubts about who is going to win the war. No Chinese have any such doubts. In fact, it is the certainty of Allied victory that has changed the character of the war in China, because it has changed both the relations between China and other countries and the scope of political maneuver within China.

Before Pearl Harbor, China was trying to get as many supplies as possible from countries which were free to make their own choice between avoiding war with Japan and risking war with Japan. China's bargaining position could be phrased somewhat as follows: We are going to keep on fighting. We are not going to negotiate any halfway peace with Japan. You must deal with that determination of ours. Perhaps your trade with Japan in war materials is very profitable. Perhaps you do not want to risk war with Japan. Even so, you want to preserve your own bargaining position against Japan. You know that if the Japanese win an overwhelming victory they will never bargain with you about the balance of power in East Asia – they will just lay down the law. Therefore you dare not let your booming trade with Japan lead to an overwhelming victory. To protect your own interests, you must also let us have at least enough to keep on holding out. (Russia must be excepted from this description of China's bargaining position. The Chinese knew that the slightest advantage won by Japan increased the danger to Russia. Therefore the Russians would give the Japanese as little as they possibly could and the Chinese as much as they possibly could and would take the risk of being attacked by Japan, though they would not take the risk of attacking Japan themselves.)

After Pearl Harbor, China's bargaining position with regard to America and Britain – especially America – was completely different. It could now be phrased somewhat as follows: You are now the ones who want help against Japan. You need a continental base to supplement your naval offensive. You need as much Chinese military activity as possible in order to commit Japanese land forces and material. If you want us to go over to the offensive, you must give us artillery and you must either build up the Chinese Air Force or increase the number of your own planes in China, or both. It is true that the Burma Road has been lost, but that was not our fault. It is up to you either to substitute a "Burma Road of the Air" or to recover the old Burma Road, or both.

With regard to Russia there was also a change. From the moment of the German attack, the Russians had both to avoid a two-front war and to strengthen their position in the event that Japan should attack them. If it was to their interest not to provoke Japan, it was also to their interest not to weaken China. The acute state of emergency, however, only lasted until Pearl Harbor. From then on the Russians were relatively safe.

These changes in China's bargaining position have inevitably raised within China itself the question of a choice between two fundamentally different strategic concepts, which may be called the side-lines concept and the front-line concept. According to the sidelines concept, China should virtually "sit out" the rest of the war. Japan is going to be defeated anyhow. China cannot undertake regular offensives without artillery and tanks, which Chinese factories cannot make and China's allies have not yet provided. To improvise an offensive by extending the area of guerilla warfare and stepping up its intensity would demand too much additional sacrifice from a people which has already made much greater sacrifices than its allies and which is still containing more Japanese ground troops than America and Britain are engaging. True, a war fought only in this passive way will leave China a beneficiary of the final victory, with a voice not fully equal to those of America, Britain, and perhaps Russia in discussing the terms of peace in the Pacific; but power politics will go on after the war, as they did before, and China will have a strong bargaining position because of the need of a strong continental power in Asia to balance the otherwise unduly strong position of Russia.

The front-line concept, on the other hand, maintains that this is the time for China to make superhuman efforts to make her own share of the common victory as big as possible by helping to defeat Japan as quickly as possible. Otherwise China will miss the full reward for her long fight for independence. China dare not be satisfied with merely a legal status of equality. She desperately needs to make herself a free agent in fact. Short of this, reliance on the rivalries of other countries is a delusion; China would still be economically and politically the pawn of others. Therefore, even if a regular offensive is impossible, an improvised "people's war" must be fought; and if this involves far-reaching political concessions to the peasants, then the concessions must be made.

These two strategic concepts have political consequences which account for the recent heightening of political tension in China, and which link up with the changing composition, discussed in the last chapter, of the Kuomintang-landlord right wing in China and the Communist-democratic-United Front left wing. The balance between these two wings creates a crisis for Chiang Kai-shek himself. Can he halt the trend of the Kuomintang toward domination by the landlords? Or can he once more make the Kuomintang a coalition, by reviving and strengthening the other groups which were once powerful in it?

To evaluate the crisis, and the American interest in it, the terms in which the crisis is currently being presented in China must be considered. By far the most powerful presentation of the position of the Kuomintang and the legally constituted government in China is the one which argues that normal political negotiations are impossible with a party, like the Communist Party, which maintains an independent armed force and is prepared to resort to civil war if its political terms are not accepted. The Communists, according to this view, should first submit their armies to government control (which would of course imply the right of the government to break up or redistribute the Communist units). Only then could democratic measures be safely discussed in a normal way, as they are in the established democracies.

Until recently Communist statements of their own views were subject to heavy discount as propaganda. There were responsible Communist representatives in Chungking; but their assertions could not be checked against public knowledge of conditions in the Communist-controlled area, because that area was tightly blockaded by government troops. A few Americans and Europeans, men who were undoubtedly free of pro-Communist bias, had escaped from Japanese-controlled territory through Communist-controlled territory, but their reports, favorable to the Communists, fell somewhat short of providing *both* information about Communist-controlled territory *and* a comparison of that information with authentic information about Kuomintang-controlled territory.

Recently, however, there has been a considerable volume of reports from American newspapermen, already thoroughly acquainted with Kuomintang China, who have been allowed to visit Yenan and have traveled through considerable stretches of Communist-controlled territory. Their reports give us the following data for a comparison: —

1. The Communists hold control, or exercise the dominant influence, in a territory inhabited by more than 80,000,000 people, partly in Free China and partly behind the Japanese lines. [The Free China territory administered by the National Government contains a population of about 200,000,000, while another 170,000,000 or so are under Japanese control.]

2. The Communists have survived, and have even expanded the territory they control, not because they subdue the people by armed force, but because the people support them.

3. Basic economic conditions as to food and clothing are better in Communist-controlled China than in Kuomintang-controlled China.

4. The incidence of conscription and taxation is more equally distributed in Communist-controlled territory than in Kuomintang-controlled territory.

5. Many progressive, educated, middle-class Chinese have somehow got through the blockade into Communist territory, but not many have fled from that territory.

6. The political structure under the Communists is more nearly democratic than it is under the Kuomintang. It is a fact that governing committees and representative committees are elected, and that the Communists limit themselves to one third of the representation; whereas in Kuomintang-controlled territory it is increasingly difficult to hold a public position without joining the Kuomintang and accepting its discipline.

There are, in the much larger area controlled by the Kuomintang, a number of minor parties – very minor parties, often called "splinter parties" by the Chinese. A few representatives of these parties are appointed to organs like the People's Political Council, which has an advisory function and a limited license for free expression of opinion, but there is no right of election to any organs which have a governing or administrative function.

Representatives of the minor parties, which have no armed forces and no rights, are inclined to believe that it is only because the Communists have armed forces that people in the Communist area have political rights and liberties. They assume that if the Communists lost control of their armed forces, the people would lose their political freedom. They therefore support, as openly as it is possible for them to do so, demands for freedom to organize political parties and the right to elect members of public bodies with real functions and authority, and do not demand that the Communists should first submit to military control.

Pending the development of a larger body of knowledge about the Communist area, certain tentative conclusions can be drawn: —

The Communists have done well enough in the territory they control to stand comparison with the Kuomintang.

There is a case for negotiating a political compromise with the Communists before pressing the question of military control.

Once there is uniformity of political rights throughout China, under a government elected by the people, that government should enforce unity of military command and uniform conditions of military service.

The present tendency in America to believe that Chiang Kai-shek is "losing control" is not warranted. Political compromise would make necessary a coalition government. Not even the Communists are strong enough to nominate a candidate of their own as President of the Republic of China, and therefore Chiang Kai-shek would be nominated by all parties, which would confirm him in the position which he now holds by appointment of the Kuomintang.

It should be added that current American public

and expert opinion greatly underrates China's ability to make a comeback and to influence the winning of the war. Thus Hanson W. Baldwin has recently gone to the extreme of saying that China "is in no sense unified," and "is not now and will not soon become under Chiang or any other leader a unified nation capable of unified effort on a scale necessary to play much part in a great offensive against Japan." [1] This is nonsense. Even on the relatively small scale of the Philippines it has already been demonstrated that it makes a world of difference in fighting the Japanese if the population turns against them. China's guerillas, as well as China's regular troops, even without great increase in equipment, can greatly increase the number of casualties inflicted on the Japanese and can even recover territory from them if political morale is restored. The fact that political morale can be restored in China should never be left out of military calculations. The overwhelming majority of the people, including those who do not belong to political parties, want to recover the sense of unity and invincibility which they had in 1926 and again in 1937, which so much astonished the experts and the world. The necessary political agreements are easier to reach than they were in 1925 and 1936. The recent cabinet changes are a cautious approach to main decisions not yet made. The most important appointment is that of General Chen Cheng, new

[1] *New York Times*, Nov. 5, 1944.

Minister of War, who represents the generals and armies closest to the tradition of national unity dating from 1926.

China of course is not the only country whose prestige has undergone changes during the war. Equally important for Asia as a whole and for the balance of influences between Asia and the Western World are changes in the prestige of the imperial powers holding colonial possessions in Asia. Britain may be taken as the representative of all these powers. France is a case apart, because the restoration of a French Government in France itself involves a regrouping of political and social forces which may have novel results in colonial policy. These problems will be touched on in the next chapter.

The Dutch Empire need not here be treated separately, because it is essentially a satellite empire. It could not exist without the British Empire, and developments within it after the war will move parallel to developments within the British Empire, whether the movement be toward emancipation or toward an attempted permanent stabilization of the institution of empire.

If the Dutch Empire is a satellite the Portuguese Empire, with its main holdings in Africa and only decaying sentry boxes in Asia and the Pacific, like Macao and Timor, is a mere shadow. The Portuguese, even more lackadaisical and corrupt in their colonies than under their fascist government at home, have very little indirect influence with which to work. The Dutch, however, have developed important economic resources in their empire. Powerful financial and industrial groups in America, as well as in Britain, have invested in these resources, and working through them the Dutch can maintain a nominal Dutch colonial policy which is actually in large part the foreign policy of exported American and British capital.

During the Munich period Britain suffered an even greater loss of prestige in Asia than in Europe. It is important to recall that Munich was only the climax of a period of appeasement stretching back behind the Chamberlain administration into the Baldwin administration. During this period one of Hitler's most skillful maneuvers was to skirmish around the fringes of colonial questions without ever coming to grips with them. By so doing he induced the British to reveal that tension in Europe was only part of a complex and slowly mounting crisis that extended also throughout the colonial world and into Asia. Influential British quarters were maneuvered into giving broad hints of their willingness to re-establish Germany as a colonial empire, while Hitler tantalizingly evaded coming to terms with them.

A number of schemes were aired in this period. There was talk of the restitution of old German colonies. There was even talk of compensating Hitler with other people's colonies, like Portuguese territory in Africa, in order to avoid handing back territory which the British and French had acquired, under the Versailles settlement, as mandates. While these offers were not official, they did not need to be official to create in Asia the impression that "peace in our time" could be translated into Asiatic and colonial languages as "empire in our time." It appeared that the Conservative Party, with only incoherent opposition from the Labour Party, was permeated with a defeatism definite enough to be called a policy: it no longer believed that it could hold the empire against all comers; it clung desperately to the institution of empire; there was no part of the colonial empire which it was willing to emancipate, but in order to preserve the institution of empire it was willing to allow others to build up competitive empires, and even to surrender to them, in the colonial status, bits of territory and consignments of human beings which it was unwilling to emancipate from the colonial status.

The resultant decline of British and Dutch prestige was of the corroding kind that works under the surface when subject peoples no longer fear the strength of their masters, but still fear the local violence of the servants of their masters, the armed police and the colonial garrisons. The inner decline of prestige was revealed externally when Japan struck. Obtuse believers in the old myth that backward colonial peoples do not understand what politics is all about should look beyond the fact that colonial possessions were lost to the Japanese, and study the way in which they were lost. I do not see how it can be doubted that the colonial peoples proved their aptitude for political arithmetic in adding up the score. The score was not exactly correct, because not all the facts were known to them; but within the limits of their knowledge they computed very shrewdly.

According to the evidence before them, the war in Asia, except in China and the Philippines, did not have enough to do with the difference between freedom and subjection to make it worth their while to participate. According to the evidence at their disposal, the war was between their old masters and would-be new masters. The new masters, if they won, might turn out to be worse than the old masters; but was that a difference worth dying for? In such a situation, if the old masters are confident and strong there will always be some of the colonial subjects who will fight for them, because rewards from strong masters are tangible, while future independence, if the masters are strong, is only a distant hope. In this case the invaders appeared to be the stronger; consequently it was to them that the hasty levies of adventurers rallied. On the British and Dutch side there was enough of the habit of discipline among the mercenary colonial troops to make most of them enter battle; but nowhere was there the ardor of patriotism, the inspiration of a cause, or the passion of a "people's war."

Since then British prestige has somewhat revived, with Dutch prestige flitting after it like a rather thin shadow. The recuperation, however, is only in military prestige, and may therefore be described as partly a token of respect to the British and Dutch as people who have powerful allies. Politically, neither the British nor the Dutch can ever hope to restore a colonial "loyalty" which never really existed. This alone means that even if the colonial structure is outwardly restored after the war, it can never expect to have inner security. The way in which the colonial possessions were lost – including the virtual loss of Indo-China by France, before Pearl Harbor – differed from the way in which the Philippines were lost in one all-important respect. It established in the colonial possessions themselves, and throughout the rest of Asia, the conviction that the imperial powers would surrender possession of their colonies to an aggressor strong enough to take them, but would not surrender freedom to the colonial peoples and ask them to fight for it. From this we may be sure that the inference has been drawn, which we must reckon with in Asia after the war, that where freedom is not planned for, as in the Philippines, the unfree peoples have no hope but to take freedom for themselves.

One way of rating the prestige of any country is to compare what it does with what it says. With

Russia, more than with any other country, what is done counts relatively more and what is said relatively less. What Russia says, more than what any other country says, is subject to distortion. One kind of distortion comes from those who believe that everything Russia says is the exact opposite of what she means, another kind from those who are oversubtle in their interpretation of what Russia "really" means, and another from those who accept everything that Russia says about Russian concerns as the only true gospel for other countries in their own concerns. Because of these distortions Russian prestige is relatively hazy at the end of any period in which Russian action has been confined to domestic affairs, since to most people what the Russians say they are doing about their own affairs is only propaganda, and relatively clear in any period when direct contact with other countries reveals what Russia is actually doing.

In Asia, Russia has changed in repute from being a land of instability to being a land of stability. All through the early years, and through the bitter social conflicts associated with the Five-Year Plans, industrialization, and collectivization, refugees from the Asiatic fringes of Russia fled into China's Northeastern Provinces and into Sinkiang, Afghanistan, and Iran. As industrialization passed from experiment and many local mistakes and failures to general and increasing success and prosperity, Russia began to acquire a reputation for stability, reinforced later by her firm handling of Japan, and especially her decisive repulse of Japanese incursions against her frontiers.

Americans themselves know less than anyone else how disastrously American prestige in Asia fell during the 1930's. American prestige fell because people in Asia understood better than people in America that the American method of "keeping out of war" was building up the strength of Japan and endangering the interests of America. A discount must of course be applied to the wishful thinking of many in China and elsewhere who knew that America had the power to save them, and hoped that somehow America could be persuaded to save them; but even when this discount has been made, the fact remains that the trend of events was better understood in Asia than in America, and that American prestige fell accordingly.

On the other hand America's Philippine record and policy saved American motives from being criticized as those of Britain were. People in Asia were realistic enough not to disregard the fact that tariff questions and the lobbying of special interests had an influence on America's Philippine policy; but they were also realistic enough not to lose sight of the fact that America was the only great power with a potentially rich colonial empire in which the alignment of special interest was not in support of the retention of empire.

It was because of our Philippine policy, and the joint defense – not colonial defense – in which

Americans and Filipinos fought side by side, that America did not suffer the loss of political prestige that Britain and Holland suffered, though Pearl Harbor was as hard a blow to our military prestige as the fall of Singapore was to that of the British. Our military prestige has long ago recovered, our political prestige — and this ought to be a matter of much more serious concern to all Americans than it is to most Americans — is undergoing a sharper scrutiny than ever before.

Our political prestige, and our political motives, are under scrutiny because they are involved with the prestige and the motives of our allies. It is perhaps possible that after the war in Europe has been won, Britain would have enough strength to spare to recover her still occupied Asiatic possessions and those of the Dutch without our aid, leaving us to attack Japan in her home waters. The war is not being fought that way, however. It is a coalition war, and because it is fought as a coalition war the overwhelming majority of people in Asia will believe that we are largely, perhaps primarily, responsible for the restoration of the British and Dutch Empires east of India, and of French rule over Indo-China if it is restored.

Our prestige is now linked as closely with the prestige of others as our policies interact with the policies of others. The last three chapters of this book will in large part be devoted to these associative relationships.

CHAPTER VI

THE POLITICS OF ATTRACTION

It is often assumed that when several nations have a large degree of control but none has full control, the balance between them will take the form of rivalry (or agreement) in setting up geographical and political spheres of interest and regions of control. In Asia after this war, however, little nations and weak peoples will still be able to have policies of their own. They will have some degree of option in deciding in which direction they themselves prefer to gravitate, especially if they stand in a geographical zone marginal to the influence of more than one great power.

Korea is an example. At the end of the war, Korea will lie within the range of American air and naval power, and will be a desirable field of operations for American economic activities. Korea will also stand under the very shadow of the Soviet Union; and finally Korea in social and economic structure is more similar to China than to any other country and has many ties of sympathy with China. How far can we assume that the actual date and circumstances of Korean independence will be disposed of simply by agreement among China, Russia, Britain, and America? How soon will the Koreans themselves form their own ideas about what they need and what they want?

Is it not reasonable to assume that they will very soon form their own estimate of the character of American, Russian, and Chinese policy? Will they not make very realistic comparisons between what we do and what we say?

There are 23,000,000 Koreans. They are one of the most homogeneous peoples in the world, and they live in a compact, sharply defined geographical area. They are thinking politically right now, and conditions after the war will give them political experience very fast. It is absurd to assume that they will not quickly try to edge over in the direction which gives them the best advantage. Korea's supposed political immaturity may prove to be largely an illusion. The real question is: What are our own political characteristics going to be?

Similar problems are scattered all through the wide geographical margins between the main centers of power. In attempting to deal with them, we must take note of the fact that the limits of influence are not always the same as the limits of control. A country may not be able to back up its control by force beyond a certain geographical limit, and still be able to exert a great influence beyond that limit if – and this "if" will be of incalculable significance in political maneuver after the war – it can exercise political attraction over the peoples with which it is dealing.

Russia, America, and China are the three nations which most clearly have a power of political attraction. They are not identical in this respect, but they are comparable. In addition, France may emerge as the war ends with a similar power of attraction. Each of these nations owes its power to attract primarily to its own behavior, rather than to its propaganda; which means that the power to attract has to be built up rather slowly and continuously, but can be lost very rapidly. The power of attraction of any one country can also vary a great deal in different regions.

In Asia, the Soviet Union has a major power of attraction, backed by a history of development and a body of precedents.

There was one striking difference between Tsarist Russia and all other colonial empires. Russia's Asiatic possessions were not divided from it by sea, but formed part of the same vast stretch of land in which lay Russia proper. The Russians were therefore in contact with their conquered subjects as a whole people, not merely through an overseas class of administrators and managers of colonial enterprises. When the Revolution broke out, it involved at the same time and in interaction with each other both those who had been masters and those who had been subjects or powerless minorities.

Because of this interaction the Bolshevik Revolution, especially in Asia, was a triple process of disintegration, integration, and reintegration. The revolutionaries, needing every ally they could attract to make possible the overthrow of tsarism, resorted to disintegration of the imperial structure by proclaiming equality of political rights for all subject and minority peoples. These peoples then integrated themselves into new political units of their own, according to their numbers, the size of their territory, the extent of their resources, and other factors which condition the ability of any people to live unto itself.

On the basis of this new integration there then began the process of reintegration into a federative Soviet Union. This was not done all at once or by decree. From 1918 to 1924 there was a complicated grouping and regrouping. The Russian Soviet Federal Socialist Republic was from the beginning the major unit. Other republics split off from it, but made agreements of various kinds with it and with each other. After a number of preliminary steps, not all of them simultaneous, the main Russian Republic combined with about six other republics to form the Soviet Union, whose first constitution was approved in 1924.

In Central Asia the process took longer. The former "native states" of Khorezm (Khiva) and Bukhara, for instance, first drove out their hereditary Emirs and set up republics which were "soviet," but not "socialist." A "soviet republic," in the terminology of those regions at that time, meant simply a democratic republic governed by elected soviets or councils. Private property and peonage continued. The landlords were the ascendant political group, reinforced by the corporate landlordism of Mohammedan religious foundations. Revolutionary groups were smothered for some years; partly because the conservatives were better organized, partly because the conservatives also joined popular groups in large numbers in order to vote down their proposals.

It was not until after the Soviet Union had been formed in 1924 that Bukhara and Khorezm voted to become socialist and applied to join the Soviet Union. Their application was accepted in 1924 and ratified in 1925, and they became the Republics of Uzbekistan and Turkmenia.

They were influenced in their decision by the Soviet power of attraction for the majority of the people. Survival at that time was uncertain for small, independent nations lying in Asia and within reach of the conflict going on in the 1920's between imperialism and nationalistic revolution. The Soviet land policy attracted the peasant majority and undermined the traditional authority of the landlords. At the same time the Soviet nationality policy was reassuring. It gave to minority peoples both freedom to be different from the Russians in such things as language and cultural habits, and freedom to be like the Russians, and equal to them, in such things as military and administrative service and industrial and technical development. The propaganda of what the Russians were actually doing in their own territory had a far more powerful effect of attraction in adjacent territory than any propaganda of theories; people who could not have been attracted by the abstract and invisible Marx were attracted by the concrete and visible Marxists.

The Russian policies were not "soft," although the Soviet Union was still weak and still threatened on all sides. They were "hard," in the sense that they were the result of a hard-boiled decision to stake the future of the Revolution on the power of attraction as a political factor. The argument was presented by Stalin himself, in his "Report on the National Question" to the Twelfth Congress of the Russian Communist Party in 1923. It was typical of Stalin, even at this early date, that he relied on performance within Soviet territory, not on propaganda abroad, even though, like other Communists at that time, he was discussing the possibility of a quick collapse of world imperialism: —

> . . . The entire Orient regards our Union as an experimental field. Either we correctly decide and practically apply the national question within the framework of this Union . . . and then the entire Orient will see that in our federation it possesses a banner of liberation, a vanguard in whose footsteps it should

walk, and this will be the beginning of the collapse of world imperialism. Or we, the entire federation, commit a mistake here, undermine the confidence of the formerly oppressed peoples in the proletariat of Russia, shear the Union of its power to attract the Orient which it now enjoys, in which event imperialism will gain and we shall lose.

The process has not stopped. The Asiatic frontier of the Soviet Union is the longest land frontier in the world. From Korea and the Northeast Provinces of China (Manchuria) past Mongolia, Sinkiang, Afghanistan, and Iran all the way to Turkey it has a double function. It divides different peoples from each other but it also separates similar people from each other. There are many Koreans and Chinese in Soviet territory (though most of the Koreans have been moved to Central Asia). Side by side with the independent Republic of Outer Mongolia there is the Associate Soviet Socialist Republic of Buryat-Mongolia; and there is another Mongol Republic far away on the lower Volga. In the Chinese Province of Sinkiang the Chinese form at most 10 per cent of the population; the Uighurs, who form 70 to 80 per cent, are rather more closely related to the Uzbeks of Soviet Uzbekistan than the Slovaks are to the Czechs. In this province there are also Kazakhs, Kirghiz, and a few Tajiks related to identical peoples in Soviet territory, and Mongols closely related both to the

Mongols of the Altai Aimak (Province) of Outer Mongolia and to the Kalmuk Mongols of the lower Volga. In Afghanistan, Iran, and Turkey there are also kindred peoples on both sides of the political frontier.

To all of these peoples the Russians and the Soviet Union have a great power of attraction. In their eyes – rather doubtfully in the eyes of the older generation, more and more clearly in the eyes of the younger generation – the Soviet Union stands for strategic security, economic prosperity, technological progress, miraculous medicine, free education, equality of opportunity, and democracy: a powerful combination.

The fact that the Soviet Union also stands for democracy is not to be overlooked. It stands for democracy because it stands for all the other things. Here in America we are in the habit of taking a narrow view of foreign claimants to the status of democracy. If China, or Russia, or some other alien people does not measure up to the standards of the particular American modification of Anglo-Saxon democracy, we say that it is not democratic. We are going to find ourselves boxing with shadows instead of maneuvering in politics if we stick to this habit. The fact is that for most of the people in the world today what constitutes democracy in theory is more or less irrelevant. What moves people to act, to try to line up with one party or country and not with another, is the difference between what is more democratic and less democratic in practice.

Doubts in America about the extent to which the Stalin constitution has really been put into effect, or criticisms of Soviet labor unions on the ground that they are not really labor unions, do not lead us anywhere in trying to understand what democracy means to people in Asia – or in the Soviet Union, for that matter. Wendell Willkie describes a "hot colloquy" on the subject of freedom with a Soviet factory superintendent. They could not get together on the subject of freedom of opinion, and finally Mr. Willkie said, "Then actually you've got no freedom." To which the Soviet engineer replied, "almost belligerently," that he had more freedom than his own father and grandfather – illiterate peasants, bound to the soil, with no medical attention when they were sick. He himself had had, from the Soviet system, an education and a chance to make good. That, for him, meant freedom.[1]

We must gear our minds to this kind of comparison if we are to understand the realities of politics in Asia. Let us take an Uighur in Sinkiang Province. He lives in a village where all the people are Uighurs; but they are ruled over by the Chinese. An Uighur may become headman of the village, but only by appointment of the Chinese authorities,

[1] Wendell Willkie, *One World*. Simon & Schuster, New York, 1943, p. 68.

not by election of the Uighurs of the village. If the Chinese authorities open a village school, it is in order to teach Chinese; if there is any propaganda allowed, it is aimed at persuading the Uighurs to stop considering themselves Uighurs and learn to be Chinese. There is no doctor in the village. There are practically no public services in return for the taxes paid.

If this Uighur learns – and he has ways of learning – that among his near kinsmen the Soviet Uzbeks, a poor man's children may attend, free, a school at which they are taught in their own language and taught to take pride in their own history and culture; that they may go on to the university and become doctors, engineers, anything in the world; that they may be elected to powerful positions in which they can give orders even to Russians, because Uzbeks and Russians are equal and it depends on a man's position, not his race, whether he gives orders – then he is going to think that the Uzbeks are free and have democracy. If he is then told that in distant America nobody considers that there is either freedom or democracy in the Soviet Union, he is going to shrug his shoulders. He is not in contact with the American system, and for him it forms no basis of action.

In Asia, the most important example of the Soviet power of attraction beyond Soviet frontiers is in Outer Mongolia. It is here that we should look for evidence of the kind of attraction that Russia might offer to Korea in the future. Outer Mongolia may be called a satellite of Russia in the good sense; that is to say, the Mongols have gravitated into the Russian orbit of their own accord (and partly out of fear of Japan and China); they have neither been subjected to a military conquest nor sold to the Russians by traitors among their own people. They have gone through their own revolution. They have taken away the titles, revenues, and powers of the hereditary princes and aristocrats; but the sons and daughters of these aristocrats are full citizens with full equality of opportunity, including government service. They have disestablished the Lama-Buddhist Church as a corporate institution owning land and other property and enjoying immunity from taxation and civil law; but they have not outlawed religion – the butter lamps burn before the shrines in the majority of tent encampments. They have begun to develop state-owned industries; but they have not abolished private property – men and women may own, buy, and sell the cattle which are the chief form of wealth in Mongolia and may hire herdsmen to tend them. Land is in a special category. Individual title to land did not exist in Mongolia even before the revolution. Formerly the land was collectively owned by the tribe, and individual use of it was allotted by the tribal rulers; now it is owned, and its use allotted, by the state.

All of this has been done with Soviet support and

help — there is a treaty of alliance between the two countries — but without assertion of Soviet sovereignty or control. Mongol officers study in Russia, and the army is Soviet-equipped, but Mongol-commanded. There is a great difference between Outer Mongolia and the puppet state of Manchukuo. From the moment they declared the "independence" of Manchukuo in 1932, the Japanese put extreme pressure on China to recognize it. The original Mongol Revolution, on the other hand, began a little earlier than the original Chinese Revolution, and the Mongol Republic calls itself a year older than the Chinese Republic. Tsarist Russia negotiated treaties prejudicial to China's sovereignty over Outer Mongolia, but Soviet Russia, though it has a treaty of alliance with Outer Mongolia, has never tried to force China to recognize Mongol independence and has even recognized China's claim to sovereignty over the Mongols. The Soviet policy may be thus described: they have just across their frontier a people who are Mongols and who call themselves independent. Friendly relations with this country have for years covered a flank of Siberia which would otherwise have been exposed to Japanese aggression. In Outer Mongolia there are no Chinese troops or representatives of the Chinese Government. The Russians deal with the people who are in the country; but they do not make it their business to force China to recognize Mongol independence, any more than they make it their business to force the Mongols to accept Chinese rule.

Soviet policy in Outer Mongolia cannot be fairly called Red imperialism. It certainly establishes a standard with which other nations must compete if they wish to practise a policy of attraction in Asia. Russo-Mongol relations in Asia, like Russo-Czechoslovak relations in Europe, deserve careful and respectful study.

China has a greater power of attraction for the colonial countries than for the non-Chinese peoples of her own frontier territories. The Chinese maintained their independence, though they lost some of their sovereignty, during the age of European colonial conquest. Since then they have successfully defended their independence in a long and terrible war against Japan's Asiatic imperialism. In so doing they have kept it on the record that the real issue in Asia is not "Asia for the Asiatics" but Asia against all imperialism, of whatever color, and for freedom and democracy.

Cutting across China's power of attraction, however, is the unpopularity of the Chinese communities living in the colonial possessions. This is in reality a subsidiary issue, but it can easily be used to confuse the major issue. It is therefore a standard move of apologists of the colonial order to suggest that only the colonial governments can protect inexperienced peoples from the grasping Chinese. Such arguments evade the real point. The Chinese are not an intrusive factor in the colonial possessions. They are part of the colonial fabric.

Although there are a few old Chinese communities in Southeast Asia, most of them were brought into the colonial possessions by Western capital, because of their usefulness as low-paid and politically defenseless labor. Out of this imported population there evolved a stratified structure of Chinese business enterprise, with peddlers and keepers of little village shops at the bottom, moneylenders and more prosperous merchants at a higher level, and owners of rice mills, plantations, tin mines, and even bankers at the top.

As they prospered, the Chinese grew unpopular for reasons which were as much colonial as Chinese. Living in the colonies, they were able to save money under a system of law, order, and police protection; but they made their money, especially at the primary level of petty enterprise and moneylending, in a manner which had been ingrained in them under the old, despotic, arbitrary conditions of China. In the old-fashioned rural China, from which most of them came, nominal rates of profit and compound interest running from 50 to 100 per cent did not really mean that a man could expect to double his capital in a short time. Far from it. They meant that a man hoped, if he was lucky, to recover his outlay in a few months with some profit or interest to spare, but had to reckon with the failure of a high proportion of his ventures. In addition, an official might come down on him with an arbitrary levy; bandits might blackmail him or hold him for ransom; civil war or the uncertainties of the harvest might wipe him out. In the colonies he was protected; the police and the law courts helped him to collect what was due to him; but the poor, on whom he lived, turned their resentment against him, not against the colonial system.

Millions of colonial subjects were never in a position to visualize the way in which the wealth which they created as laborers, farmers, and plantation hands was shipped away to Europe and America in solid tons of cargo, in tankers loaded with oil, in the remittance of banking, shipping, insurance, and rental profits, in the salaries and bonuses of corporation officials and the pay and pensions of colonial civil servants. They were in a position to see how the Chinese operated in their own slum, village, or plantation compound. They knew how quickly a dollar of wages became two dollars of debt when they had to borrow money from a Chinese, or buy two yards of cotton cloth from him on credit. How could they be expected to understand how big-time colonial enterprise meshed with the wheels of Chinese enterprise within the colonial system? They did not know that the Chinese with whom they dealt had to pay high interest himself to the wealthier Chinese, or the guild, which financed him; that behind the middlemen lay mysterious loans and mortgages in the great stone banks of Rangoon, Singapore, or Soerabaja.

It is possible that after the war this whole system will be restored. There is also the possibility, however – in my opinion quite a high probability – that there will be great changes. Every slight improvement in political and economic conditions in China will, I believe, draw Chinese back to the homeland from the colonies. We should not forget that the colonial system was a prestige system. Many patriotic nationalistic Chinese would have gone back to China to engage in business and economic development had they not believed in the Gibraltar-like security of their savings and investments in the colonies. They universally resented the fact that in the colonies they were held down, politically, to the level of the subject peoples. The old prestige of colonial security can never be fully restored. The Chinese, therefore, are likely to feel that the basic security of China is greater than that of the colonies, and to return there in proportion to the rate at which China becomes a country attractive to the businessman; and if there is any such process, or even tendency, it can be expected to increase China's prestige and power of attraction.

In this context it seems probable that the fear of a "Chinese imperialism" in Southeast Asia is largely synthetic. Chiang Kai-shek has repudiated in strong terms the idea that China might want to assume "the mantle of an unworthy Japan," or of Western imperialism: "China has no desire to replace Western imperialism in Asia with an Oriental imperialism or isolationism of its own or of anyone else." On our own part, it is well to guard against using a hypothetical imperialism, even subconsciously, to justify the perpetuation of an imperialism which actually exists. If we are to deal in suppositions, we may well suppose that if, after the war, colonial nationalists who stay in the colonies are jailed, while those who escape to China are received with sympathy and respect, the colonial attraction toward China will be increased. It would be well for us to allow also for a quick maturing of political sophistication among the colonial peoples. They may continue to have their reservations about the Chinese who live among them and still feel that the increasing strength of a free China reinforces the contention that all Asiatics are capable of independence.

In Tibet, Sinkiang, and Mongolia there is a different situation. These territories formed, with China, part of the Manchu Empire. The Chinese, as the people who overthrew the Manchu throne, have a certain claim to its former possessions. On the other hand, there is some validity in the theory that the Manchu throne was the only link between the constituent parts of the empire, and that with the deposition of the empire each people had a right to go its own way. Most of Mongolia and most of Tibet were never conquered by the Chinese in the past. There were periods of deep Chinese penetration into Sinkiang, in the long and complex history of that region; but these periods lie far back in the past. Under the Ming Dynasty (1368–1643) which preceded the Manchu conquest of China, and later of Sinkiang, the Chinese were unable to conquer Sinkiang.

There are two primary reasons why the peoples of these regions, who are wholly un-Chinese in language and tradition, should feel attracted toward China. Either they might gravitate toward China for fear of Russia (in Mongolia and Sinkiang), or for fear of Britain (in Tibet and to a certain extent in Sinkiang). Or they might be drawn toward China by China's own social, political, and economic progress, if they were able to feel that they were being admitted to that program, not subjected to it. At the present time, they are not gravitating toward China for either reason. It is practical politics, however, to count on the possibility that China could very quickly create a power of attraction for the border peoples. China could, without going Communist, practise a minority policy with most of the characteristics of the Soviet minority policy. Here again behavior is more important than propaganda: the basic requirement is rapid and visible democratization among the Chinese themselves.

Comparison of the varying powers of attraction which one country may exercise along the frontiers or within the possessions of another country suggests that an important political principle will be at work in the postwar world. It can be worded as follows: When a country feels that its citizens or its subjects are unduly attracted toward another country, it is difficult to offset that attraction by forbidding it or making it illegal. To attempt to suppress the trend by force or police regulation is likely to increase the force of the attraction. It is therefore worth considering the political uses of counterattraction – a clearer and more rapid trend toward emancipation in the colonial possessions, a clearer and more rapid evolution of democratic processes. Against which Russia, to maintain her present comparative advantages, would have to keep up the trend toward increased personal liberty and economic prosperity which has contributed so largely to those advantages.

If the clash of power politics is in fact to be mitigated by exploiting the political uses of attraction, it is possible that France may rise from defeat to a great influence in the colonial world. France's possessions in Indo-China were infiltrated by Japan even before the war in Europe began. The French could count on little loyalty, because Indo-China had long been the most corruptly administered of their major colonies. Then France itself was overrun by the Germans, and the French possessions in Africa assumed a sudden and critical importance in the rallying of the Free French movement and preparation for recovery of the homeland.

With the expulsion of the Germans, the French have with remarkable rapidity recovered many of the elements of both power and prestige. French regulars and colonial troops took part in the invasion and have also fought in Italy. Even more important in contributing to the revival of France's political prestige was the part played by the underground. The French democratic tradition, which many thought had rotted away, has clearly proved its continuing vitality. France has not yet recovered, however, enough power either to reconquer, independently of her allies, such lost colonial domains as Indo-China, or to discuss in full equality with her allies the future of Europe.

The situation is one in which the French may be impelled to increase their prestige as a method of recovering further power, instead of waiting for the recovery of power to rebuild prestige. They may, in fact, take the lead over both America and Britain in deliberately exploiting policies of attraction, by making France the main center for the rebuilding of democratic practices in Western Europe. If, by so doing, they can create a pressure which will help to bring their position more nearly up to that of America and Britain in Europe, they may also find it expedient to put attraction rather than force in the forefront of their attempt to rebuild their colonial empire. There are already signs of such possibilities in French discussion of colonial problems and methods.[2] It is quite possible that by

[2] See two articles by Pierre Olivier Lapie: "The Future of New Caledonia," *Pacific Affairs*, Sept. 1944; and "The New Colonial Policy of France," *Foreign Affairs*, Oct. 1944.

a policy of federalization, rights of citizenship, free access to French culture combined with freedom to develop non-French cultural heritages, and full economic freedom to initiate agreements with all countries, France could combine the flow of the democratic trend in Europe and in the colonies, and set a standard which other countries would find it hard to oppose both at home and in their colonies.

America has at present the clearest power of attraction for all Asia. We have a unique reputation for good faith, because we not only promised freedom to the Philippines but set a date for that freedom. For this one reason our liberation policy is accepted as genuine, while the vague promises to other colonies of "self-government," or "dominion status," at some time in an unspecified future, but not freedom in one word, are subject to the discount of an obstinate suspicion.

We have the advantage of standing for democratic processes of government under a republican form of government. Colonies of countries under monarchical governments universally aspire to become republics. Moreover in a colony which is under a monarchy the principle of monarchy becomes a point of support for native princes, rajahs, and all those groups with hereditary privileges among the colonial people themselves who are most opposed to progress and most frightened by the idea of independence.

We have also the advantage of being regarded as

the country in which, while the workingman has rights and safeguards, the businessman has unlimited opportunities. We are therefore specially attractive to the business group which is so potent in colonial nationalism, because it wants not only political freedom but freedom from the tariffs, taxation schedules, and banking practices which in colonial systems work against native industry and trade and in favor of the big interests operating at long range from the home countries.

A power of attraction is not, however, in itself a policy of attraction. In order to practise a policy, there must be an objective. We are open to the criticism of having no clear positive war aims; but at least negatively one thing is clear: we are not in search of territories in Asia to annex. It may be added that our power of attraction differs from that of Russia and China in one important respect: we are not in contact by land with the Asiatic regions for which we have the quality of attraction.

Since we are not in contact by land, and since there is no question of annexation, we could adopt a policy of attraction only for the purpose of encouraging the development of nations which are similar to us in being independent, and similar enough to us in political, social, and economic structure to promote investment and trade on terms which are mutually profitable, and which do not represent unequal economic exploitation by us. If we adopt such a policy, it will be facilitated by the power of attraction which we already have. If we do not, our present power of attraction will rapidly fade.

Britain and Holland, in dealing with their own colonial subjects, have little of that quality of attraction which has here been discussed. Nevertheless Britain has a considerable power of retention; and so does Holland, to the extent that it can work with Britain as a junior partner in the recovery of colonial territories. If we consider simply the power to act and the will to act, it should not be too difficult to re-establish colonial rule. The Japanese have everywhere identified themselves as new colonial rulers, not as liberators. As they are pressed back, their prestige will everywhere disintegrate. The prestige of the colonial powers will recover correspondingly. It will not be a prestige that includes much respect or liking; but it will not need to be.

Resistance to the returning masters will probably be scattered and light, because there will be no armed populations to repress. There will be resentment and passive resistance; but colonial administrators are experienced in dealing with these manifestations. If a few key political organizers are killed in a cold and orderly manner, with the right kind of harsh insistence that they are troublemakers and the right kind of blank refusal to discuss the possibility that patriotism could have anything to do with their behavior; if at the same time the right kind of quislings are forgiven — those who once worked for the old masters just because they were the masters, then served the Japanese just because they were the new masters, and are willing to switch their honest services back to the old masters as soon as they return; and if transport, food supply, and tax gathering are quickly reorganized, it should not be very difficult to restore colonial law and order.

If this is what is to happen, we shall be involved in it, even if we think we are not. We must not fool ourselves into thinking that people in colonial Asia do not know what kind of war this is. We can be sure that even among the illiterate and the politically inexperienced it will be widely known that victory over Japan is a coalition victory. To that victory the British will make a large contribution, because they have arms, planes, ships, and significant numbers of men of their own. The Dutch, who were able to salvage little but money from either Holland or their Asiatic Empire, have few men and have to borrow their prestige where they borrow or buy their armament. America's own naval, air, and land forces, and American equipment used by America's allies, will be in the forefront in driving out the Japanese. Therefore, even if we should declare that we have no policy toward other people's colonies, the colonial peoples will enter to our account a large measure of credit or blame, according to the degree in which victory over Japan works out as colonial liberation or colonial reconquest.

Where does our interest lie? First of all, I think,

we must recognize that we cannot wholly divorce moral issues and practical methods. It is true that for the British as for us there is a moral issue as between continuing or bringing to an end the institution of colonial empire. It is true that colonialism is a kind of slavery – the ownership of one group of people by another. It is also true, however, that British and Dutch needs, as well as interests, are much more closely integrated with the colonial system than our needs and interests were ever integrated with the Philippines. We must remember also that the colonial system is the product of a long historical growth. The British and the Dutch cannot simply declare themselves out of it. They can only get out of it by a planned policy which takes care of the consequences at home as well as in the colonies.

Whatever they do, and whether they take the initiative in order to better their own interests or are forced to adjust themselves to a general trend which they cannot control, they must adjust their home economy to their colonial policy. The British, especially, must think of thousands of senior civilian and military appointments, hundreds of thousands of military and naval enlisted personnel and white-collar jobs, and millions of factory jobs. Our own investment and trade interests are involved in this problem, because they extend into Britain, and to a lesser extent into Holland and France, as well as into the colonies of all three countries.

An approach to the handling of the problem can be suggested by comparing colonial economy as it is with the economic structure that could be encouraged in colonial regions politically liberated under a planned and orderly program. Strategically important but militarily weak areas, especially in the tropics and subtropics, as we know from our own experience in the Caribbean and Latin America, are the natural prey of cartels and monopolies. Special interests of this kind can easily be represented as national interests and can have a powerful influence in determining whether the State Department sends a note, or the Navy sends a squadron, or the Marines land. It is a salutary thing for us to remember, when offering advice about Asia, that this is the reason why we have so little power of attraction in Latin America, where in fact we are widely feared and often hated.

Colonial Southeast Asia and the Southwest Pacific produce things like tin, rubber, oil, quinine, hemp and other fibers, coconut oil, and tea which have a fatal tendency to be tied up by monopolies within nations which combine with each other to form cartels of private interests between nations. If our public interest resigns itself to a policy of drift, groups which are alive to their own special interests can easily convert that drift into a form of private policy disguised as national policy. We could easily find ourselves committed to pseudo-national policies which would actually represent national support for groups within our own nation acting as the long-range backers and partners of an indefinitely prolonged colonialism. This kind of international colonialism would be under flags other than the American flag, but the people who suffered from it would detect the American backing. The result would be rapid disintegration of all our power of attraction. We should find that we had failed to detect and work with the tide of evolution. Frustrated evolution breaks out eventually in revolution; and we should find ourselves in the path of that revolution.

What kind of policy could encourage better economic results? The problem can be reduced to the following elementary factors: We have an interest in standing for colonial liberation, in order to preserve and use the power of attraction which is one of our valuable political assets. We need colonial liberation to be rapid enough to retain the confidence and good will of colonial nationalists. We need it to be orderly enough to give time for economic and social readjustment in countries which have long settled into the habit of being partly supported by colonial tribute. We need to be on guard against allowing the present colonialism to be converted into an international cartel colonialism.

As I consider these factors, it seems to me that an important step toward the solution of the problem is a policy of encouraging the development of independent local capital and industry in colonial territories. As I have already pointed out, the businessmen among the subject peoples are in the forefront of progress. They want political independence not only for itself, but as a step toward economic freedom of opportunity. To maintain their economic ascendancy among their own people, they need to be able to show that they can build up their own industry and trade. If it should become evident that they can in fact operate only as the agents and hangers-on of absentee foreign interests, then they will lose prestige among their own people and nationalistic leadership, both economic and political, will shift away from them, far to the left.

They can only build up a sound economic structure if they are allowed to set tariffs which allow them to accumulate capital and build up industries. This means that we, and the former imperial nations too, must abandon the present system under which we open up branch agencies in colonial territories to hire cheap labor, extract what we want, and ship it out. We must adapt ourselves to a system of trading on equal terms with local owners of the resources, who get out of the handling of those resources not merely wages or an agent's commission but the profits of investment.

Before going further into the details of policy, however, it is advisable to examine problems of security, and the changing setting within which politics must work – whether it is power politics, the politics of security, or the politics of attraction.

CHAPTER VII

THE POLITICAL NATURE OF SECURITY

As THE END of the war approaches it is natural that there should be a strong demand that our statesmen and military leaders should make America safe against another Pearl Harbor. It is assumed that we were vulnerable at the time of Pearl Harbor because we did not have enough power at our disposal, distributed at the right geographical points. There is a temptation, therefore, to think that we shall be secure for the future if we maintain a two-ocean navy and a large number of long-range aircraft, keep our land forces at whatever size may be necessary to match the potential competition of other big armies, and annex the Japanese Mandated Islands, and perhaps other outlying islands, like the Bonins, to make a screen of bases in the Western Pacific.

Military security is a necessary part of a stable peace; but military security alone cannot assure the safety of a nation which is confused in its political thinking. On the other hand, a nation which is clear in its political thinking can overcome the handicap of military weakness to a surprising extent. The

Chinese were able to stall the onrush of the Japanese and force a long war on them because, in spite of differences between the Kuomintang and the Communists, both parties understood the approaching danger and adjusted themselves to it. Whereas the response to President Roosevelt's appeal to "quarantine the aggressors" in 1937 proved that we as a people did not understand the kind of world we were living in. The speech alarmed a great part of the public and was howled down by the press. From then on it was impossible for the President to coordinate an American foreign policy properly balanced between Asia and Europe. Foreseeing war, but without enough backing to enable him to make adequate preparations, he had to edge in the direction in which maneuver was least obstructed, which meant cautious preparation to support Britain. Hampered as he was by the public's timidity in supporting even this cautious and conditional policy, it was impossible for him to formulate an inclusive policy based on the combined realities of Europe and Asia. Russia, the link between Europe and Asia, had to be treated as if the potentialities of enmity were a pressing menace, and the potentialities of friendship illusory. Such aid as could be given to China was channeled through Treasury policy, in the form of loans, rather than through State Department policy.

Our most urgent problem after the war will still be the integration of political security with military security. In fact, the co-ordination of policy with strategy is already a problem in the conduct of the war. In Europe, the United Nations have already worked out a common strategy and are moving closer together on the terms of peace settlement. In Asia, there is not as yet a common strategy, and one reason for the delay in strategic agreement is the failure to reach a reasoned agreement on the Asiatic political settlement. In other words, the fact that we have fallen short in the sphere of policy is delaying victory.

After the war, if we are determined to prevent another Pearl Harbor, we must take into account more than the fact that December 7, 1941, happened to be a Sunday on which we were caught off guard; we must also avoid the kind of thinking which led up to a situation in which we were predisposed to be caught off guard. We had allowed the Japanese, and in fact helped them, to build up a situation so favorable to themselves that even if we had been on the alert at Pearl Harbor, had saved our own fleet and destroyed the attacking planes, the enemy might quite possibly have extricated their task force, kept the over-all initiative, and taken Guam, the Philippines, Hong Kong, Singapore, Netherlands India, and Burma. We had thought, in our dealings with the Japanese before Pearl Harbor, that we were realists who could trade with anyone at a profit because we controlled an invaluable something known as the Balance of Power. Because of this invaluable something we could safely let the

Japanese gouge bits out of China and still be sure of restraining them from taking over China outright. They might attack Russia, with us in their rear; but they would never be so foolhardy as to attack us, with Russia in their rear, and an unfinished war in China, and the British at Singapore. With a large part of our nation permeated by this kind of thinking, we practically put a sign on Pearl Harbor as a good place to go to sleep.

America can take over the positions held by Japan in the Mandated Islands and elsewhere in the Pacific and set up a row of Pearl Harbors far west of Hawaii. The British, Australians, and New Zealanders can fortify their own Pacific island positions. The Russians also have already, or can take, the bases necessary for a strong combination of land, sea, and air power. In addition the Chinese can, in time, fortify very strong positions on their own coast and in Formosa. We could thus redistribute the former Anglo-American-Japanese balance of power and assure ourselves against a renewal of Japanese aggression; but this is not the only problem. We cannot deal with the future simply by dividing and redistributing the Asia and Pacific of the past. It is even more important to provide for the changes which are bound to come in Asia, in such a manner as to make power conflicts unnecessary.

In destroying Japan's military power we must not overlook the fact that Japan industrially is like Italy and unlike Germany in its dependence on external sources of raw materials. Military defeat alone will not automatically make Germany a second-class industrial power; but Japan, with the loss of Formosa, Korea, and China's Northeastern Provinces (Manchuria), will automatically become a third-class industrial power.

Industrial growth in Asia, however, will continue, first in China and Soviet Asia and later in other regions. The total industrial horsepower just west of Japan, on the mainland of Asia, will soon exceed that of Japan at the time of Pearl Harbor. Between Lake Baikal and Vladivostok oil, coal, iron, hydroelectric power, timber, and a number of metals are all available without drawing on the Urals or any other region. The Soviet Far East is already manufacturing both heavy products like ships and locomotives and refined equipment like machine tools and airplane engines. China will not reach the same stage of development with the same speed; but within fifty years China, with a far greater and better balanced supply of raw materials in her own territory than Japan ever had, can have a better rounded industry than that of Japan today.

With industrial development of this order of magnitude on the mainland of Asia, advanced bases on islands taken from Japan would not give us control of the balance of power. It is particularly dangerous to exaggerate the importance of island air bases. If Asia were to remain colonial and unindustrialized, our planes could give us the kind of advantage that the Italians had over the Abyssinians. If the Chinese and Russians were incapable of developing a better air industry than that of Japan today, we could count on an air superiority similar to that which we now have over Japan. But we cannot count on a permanently backward Asia, and therefore if we can think of no approach to the Western Pacific except that of power politics, we must resign ourselves to the fact that the Western Pacific lies closer to the future industrial production and air and naval bases of the Asiatic mainland than to those of the North American mainland.

The power of America, Britain, and Russia to set up purely military standards of security at the end of the war is therefore not in itself an assurance of lasting peace. The redistribution of military power could either lead up to a future opposition between great powers or it could prepare the way for an organized system of lasting peace. In choosing between these alternatives, political thinking is even more important than military planning.

Problems of this kind were the subject of the Dumbarton Oaks Conference for planning a future world organization. The Conference produced a draft charter for a future United Nations organization, to include more than the present United Nations and to succeed the League of Nations. The organization would include a Security Council of eleven. Permanent seats would be held by America, Britain, China, Russia, and "in due course" France.

Six elective seats would be held for two-year terms by smaller countries. The Conference, at the time of publishing the draft charter, was unable to agree on voting procedure. It has been reported that Russia proposed that each of the permanent members – the most powerful countries – should have the power of veto; and that a member of the Security Council, even if accused of aggression, should be entitled to vote on the question.

Since the proposal was attributed to Russia, the policy has been discussed as Russian; but it may be conceded that even if Russia had not made the proposal, some similar ruling would have to be included in the final charter if it is to be ratified by the American Senate, owing to the strong American reluctance to surrender sovereignty. The proposal has been criticized as running counter to fundamental ideas of justice, because any permanent member of the Security Council would, if accused of aggression, be able to take part in judging the accusation, and to veto a majority vote ruling the accusation justifiable. Injustice and aggression, however, are things that begin at various stages along the whole course of this process; to preserve a stable peace, they should be eliminated or stopped as nearly as possible at the stage at which they originate. If an inequitable policy is allowed to develop into open aggression, and to become so serious that it has to go all the way up to a Security Council at the apex of an international organization, then in all probability the votes cast will not result in justice, but will separate the great powers, each with its attendant smaller nations, into the two sides that will sooner or later fight a next war.

If our real interest is in the working organization of a stable peace, rather than in maneuvering for a favorable position in a next war, then it is worth our while to concentrate on the possibilities of the lower, earlier stages of the process of international relations, rather than on the dramatic possibilities of the great powers in the top Security Council. The Dumbarton Oaks draft charter provides, for instance, for a Court of International Justice which "should function in accordance with a statute which should be annexed to and be a part of the charter of the [United Nations] Organization." This would provide a forum for disputes which are legal in the proper sense of the word, leaving to the Security Council decisions which are essentially political.

The draft charter also provides for a General Assembly, with representation of all members of the enlarged United Nations. It is unfortunate that the General Assembly was dismissed, by some of the early commentators, as "a mere debating society," since its functions could in fact be made very flexible and comprehensive. Among its many functions, it would be empowered to set up an Economic and Social Council "with a view to the creation" – not merely with a view to the maintenance – "of conditions of stability and well-being which are necessary for peaceful and friendly relations among nations"; and there would also be "various specialized economic, social and other organizations." We have, in short, already reached a stage of statesmanlike international political thinking which is ready to provide many cross references and alternatives of procedure. Disputes, claims, and aspirations which, if neglected, would tend to force the choosing of sides for a future war could be handled at an early stage. They could be brought to the Economic and Social Council before going on to the General Assembly, or to the International Court of Justice before going on to the Security Council; or the Security Council, having had a case referred to it directly, could before taking action first refer the case to the Court of International Justice, and so on. The Economic and Social Council could, among other important possibilities, become a court of first reference and clearinghouse for colonial countries, dependent peoples, and minorities.

The Dumbarton Oaks draft charter is in fact an encouragingly realistic document. In outlining the functions of the Security Council it recognizes the fact that while the concept of equality is important, equality of power does not exist. It therefore makes the responsibility of America, Britain, and Russia as conspicuous as their power, and to these three nations it adds China and France, which stand on the threshold of achieving comparably great power. At the same time, by providing a variety of channels for the flow of international relations, it recognizes that even the greatest powers are not omnipotent. These channels can be made to serve quite as efficiently in concentrating pressure on the great powers from many sources as in distributing the influence of the great powers in many directions.

A wholly satisfactory world organization cannot be perfected on the drafting board. It must be tested and improved under working conditions; and under working conditions we are likely to find that nations whose political and power potentials are hard to foretell will have a decisive influence. If they are provided with a framework firm enough to give them support but adaptable enough to allow them to grow and mature, and if they show the capacity to grow into this framework and fill it, then organization for peace can successfully replace division between rival power groupings.

In Asia the key countries in this respect will be China, Outer Mongolia, Korea, the Philippines, and Thailand, which will constitute a freedom bloc. Each of these countries – even China – will be weak in strategic power, industry, and political integration as compared with America, Britain, and Russia, the three giants. As a bloc they will stand between the three giants and the unsatisfied millions of unfree Asia. Individually, each of them will be tested in its own capacity to show stability and assume responsibility; and at the same time, both individually and as a group, they will serve as a test of the political integrity and aptitude for co-operation of the three giants.

Within this freedom bloc China, already rated officially as a fourth giant power, will be of overwhelming importance. As China goes, so goes Asia. A free China means independence for something like half the people of Asia, and therefore a strong shift in the balance between the political life of free peoples and subject peoples. If the Chinese show that they are able to move beyond old provincial traditions of separatism, and at the same time to accommodate themselves to the organized partisan rivalry of political parties, they will weaken the most deeply rooted political assumptions which maintain the imperial system in India and the Asiatic colonies. If on the other hand they reveal that they are not yet able to reconcile the organized disunity of party politics with the fundamental unity of democratic nationalism, they will fortify all the prejudices that are built into the colonial system.

There is a delicate and critical relationship between the unduly prolonged system of "political tutelage" in China, and the arbitrary discretion of colonial rulers on which conservatives rely for the prolongation of the colonial order. In hastening the solution of these interconnected problems the power of decisive action lies with the Chinese, and within China with the Kuomintang. If, by the time the war ends, the Chinese already have the right to organize under more than one party and to elect representatives to responsible office, then in the more advanced colonial regions, like India and Java, it will be difficult to continue "colonial trusteeship" except on a relatively short-term basis. If the war ends with an increasingly unpopular one-party tutelage still imposed on an increasingly unwilling and restive Chinese people, then the advocates of colonial trusteeship will justify a long-term retention of the colonial order on the ground that the Asiatic people which has had the best opportunity has not shown itself able to cope with the realities of democratic life.

Moreover, the direction taken by China may determine the fate of Japan for many decades. In proximity to a democratically progressive China, the evolution of democracy in Japan would be relatively easy. A politically retarded China would also be economically retarded and undermined by rural poverty and discontent; China's allies would feel the lack of support for a co-ordinated policy strong and assured enough to allow latitude for experiment, and in America and Britain, at least, this would result in demands for a long-range, authoritarian, quasi-colonial control of Japan.

China's importance, great though it is, must not be allowed to hide from view the importance of the other countries of the freedom bloc.

Thailand, wedged between British and French colonial possessions and a close neighbor of China, was a free country before the war. Sir Josiah

Crosby, a British advisor to the Thai Government before the war, however, maintains that Thailand should be reduced to tutelage for an indefinite period, because its rulers proved "irresponsible" during the period of the rise and aggression of Japan.[1]

Irresponsibility, however, is not an absolute quality, and it would be extremely dangerous to discriminate between European irresponsibility and Asiatic irresponsibility. The Thai people, in the setting of Asia, are as politically mature as the Rumanian people in the setting of Europe. The Thai rulers were no more irresponsible than the rulers of Rumania. To suspend Thai independence but not that of Rumania would imply racial discrimination to all Asiatics, both free and subject. Tutelage over Thailand would be very detrimental to our prestige, because it could not be imposed without our assent. Even a temporary tutelage over Thailand would be taken as a maneuver to expand imperialism in practice while talking in theory about emancipation out of imperialism. Everywhere in Asia the word "temporary" is suspect when it is associated with an extension of European control. The nation which assumed tutelage over Thailand would be regarded as attempting to add a part of Japan's imperial sphere to its own imperial sphere.

[1] "Observations on a Post-War Settlement in South-East Asia," by Sir Josiah Crosby, K.C.M.G., K.D.E., *International Affairs,* London, July, 1944. (Address given at Chatham House on June 1, 1943.)

In the past, America was always hopefully regarded as the country which might check Japan; but American assent to tutelage over Thailand would be taken as proof that we were opposed to Asiatic imperialism but are now not opposed to European imperialism.

Our most direct concern within the freedom bloc in Asia is with the Philippines. The welcome we have been receiving since General MacArthur's return to the Philippines is, however, of as much concern to our colony-owning allies as it is to us. The fact that we are succeeding in recovering the Philippines before the British, Dutch, and French recover their possessions will affect the whole character of the war in Asia. When British prestige in Asia was being roughly handled by the Japanese, before Pearl Harbor, Mr. Quo Tai-chi, then Chinese Ambassador in London, was asked what he thought. "I think," he replied, "that the sky is black with chickens coming home to roost." Black though the sky was then, there are still more chickens to come.

Apathy and even hostility in the colonial possessions, contrasting with the welcome for the Americans in the Philippines, confront our allies with difficult problems; but the fact that we have been welcomed in the Philippines does not mean that we are going to be free of problems. The Philippines Government in Exile has remained in closer touch and sympathy with its people than any other government in exile; but even so, President Osmeña and the Americans who brought him back must deal with new political forces which have developed during the years of Japanese occupation. Among the guerillas and in the resistance movement in areas under Japanese occupation new leaders have made their mark, and their followers represent political forces. The landlord problem is as important in the Philippines as it is elsewhere in Asia. In the Philippines, as elsewhere, property owners have tended to be cautious for fear of losing their property, while peasants and the common people have been the unfailing reservoir of courage in non-co-operation and boldness in action.

Among the Filipinos, moreover, as among the Chinese who also have a stake in an actual and visible freedom, there is a vivid sense of community of interest with the peoples who are not yet free. The belief throughout Asia that freedom is indivisible is as important as the conviction all over the world that peace is indivisible. While we are fearful of setting people free before they are strong enough to walk alone, all Asia is convinced that the trend toward emancipation must continue as a steady, uninterrupted process, and intensely suspicious of any attempt to freeze this process at the immediate postwar level for a "cooling-off" period. Our conduct in the Philippines will accordingly influence opinions about our democratic character all over Asia; the primary essential is that our policy should avoid using individuals as "chosen instruments" – the policy which has made us so unpopular in Latin America – but should welcome and adapt itself to a widening participation in political life by the people as a whole.

At the Cairo Conference America, Britain, and China declared for the independence of Korea "in due course." The manner in which we implement this pledge will be important for the whole freedom bloc in Asia as a test of whether we believe in people or in rulers of the people, in democracy or in the principle of *Fuehrers* and *Gauleiters*. The 23,000,000 Koreans have been under an alien police terror since 1910. Only those over forty-five or fifty can remember independence. The rest have not had even such limited means of presenting claims, or registering objections, as exist in India. There are no visible political organizations, and even underground organizations are probably fragmentary. There is no way of computing the number of people who support any group or movement. Political action, as in the blackest days of repression in Ireland, has been reduced to the habit of sporadic terrorism, which is a bad form of training for government.

Outside of Korea there are several groups of exiled leaders. They have been exiled for so long that none of them would automatically be accepted as leaders or representatives by whatever underground movements may exist. They are in fact claimants with rival programs rather than leaders of competing followings. If we should arbitrarily attempt to impose one of these groups and its program we should make ourselves unpopular very quickly. Our political record up to the present shows that in some ways we are the most timidly conservative of all the United Nations. We tend to put our money, in liberated territories, on men whom we call moderate but whom their own people, all too often, call reactionary.

In Korea this will not do. It is as nearly certain as anything in politics can be that when the lid is taken off, the long-repressed political instincts of the Korean people will boil over in many factional movements. They will undoubtedly quarrel with each other, but undoubtedly the major tendency will be both fiercely nationalistic and radical. Like all other colonial peoples, the Koreans are in the main a peasant people. As in most of colonial Asia, the landlord class is the nearest thing to a quisling class. Some of the landlords, however, impoverished by the Japanese, will emerge as leaders of groups in sympathy with peasant needs.

Our own habits of political thinking will expose us to the danger of throwing our weight against Korean movements which we think "too radical." In the meantime both the Chinese Communists and the Russians will quickly get into touch with the few Korean Communists (as they will with the few Japanese Communists) and also with a rather wide progressive group which will fear a moderate Communist-sponsored program less than it will an immoderately conservative American program. Since we must live henceforth in a world in which Communism has become a permanent factor, and in a large part of Asia a "respectable" and progressive factor, we must allow for the fact that Korea is distant from us, and close to areas in which the Communists have a high prestige; it is to our interest that the Russians, and therefore Communism, should be associated with us, the Chinese, and the British in joint responsibility for a moderate but clearly progressive policy which will turn responsibility over to the Koreans themselves as fast as possible.

Finally, we should enlarge our acceptance of a freedom bloc in Asia to include Outer Mongolia. We need take no initiative in identifying ourselves either with the Chinese claim that Outer Mongolia is Chinese territory or with the Russian policy of recognizing Outer Mongolia as independent. The important facts for us are that Outer Mongolia has long been independent in fact and that the Chinese will not be in a position at the end of the war to conquer the Mongols by force. We shall need to have a policy, however, because there will certainly be demands for union with Outer Mongolia in the fringing territories of Inner Mongolia which are still Mongol in population. (Most of Inner Mongolia has been colonized by Chinese, and should be expected to remain Chinese.) It is not to our interest that claims and counterclaims in Mongolia should affect our friendly relations with either China or Russia. It is to our interest, therefore, that the Chinese and the Mongols should come to terms as free peoples; whether by Chinese recognition of Mongol independence or by free Mongol consent to enter a federated Chinese union does not greatly matter. Under either settlement we could come into diplomatic contact with Mongolia and engage in economic activities there, and our relations with both China and Russia, as well as the relations of China and Russia with each other, would be relieved of the awkwardness of a strategic area of nearly 700,000 square miles which in international politics is a blank to us but not to China or Russia, with which we are closely associated.

The very existence of a freedom bloc extending from the Sino-Russian frontier into the geographical area of the colonial order, and embracing both part of the Japanese Empire and territory liberated from Japanese occupation, makes it impossible to think of limiting the problems of policy by dividing up Asia into more or less permanent spheres of influence or control allotted to the greatest of the great nations. The freedom bloc exists because change is at work in Asia. Within the freedom bloc as a whole change cannot be halted or suspended. Within each of the countries of the freedom bloc the rate of change will vary. We must, therefore, adjust our minds to the necessity of shaping policy under the conditions of a long period of change.

The trend of change as a whole is toward the ending of the great historical age of imperialism. Like all major historical phases, it will not end suddenly, but by a process of transition. What matters to us is that we are involved in the process. If we were to attempt to stop it, transition would only quicken into revolution. We can, however, help to guide the transition into relatively smooth, evolutionary channels.

The details of policy in the double problem of adapting ourselves to the necessity of change, while helping change to take place in even, evolutionary stages, will be dealt with in the final chapter. Before we can deal with details, however, we must frame for ourselves a standard of reference. The essential standard is this: we are going to feel a nostalgic, emotional pull toward a return to the world as it was before Hitler and before Pearl Harbor. We shall sentimentalize the attractiveness of that world; but the world in which we are going to live will nevertheless be a world of change. Asia will condition our life and times because so much of Asia is under colonial rule and because the end of the age of imperialism will affect so large a proportion of the people of the world directly that it will affect all the rest of the world indirectly. The democratic order has been so closely intertwined with the imperial order in its origins and through the whole history of its development that it cannot remain unaltered when the imperial order ends.

We must therefore learn a lesson for which our experience has as yet imperfectly prepared us: the lesson of the closeness with which domestic policy interacts with policy abroad. The democratic order will not end when the imperial order ends, but its institutions and practices will tend to continue to change, by an unending process of transition succeeding transition. At home, as abroad, we have the choice of attempting to facilitate change by an intelligent study of evolution, or attempting to halt change entirely, in which case we shall build up the pressures that eventually break out in revolution.

We cannot count on a breathing space at the end of the war in which to pick our economic opportunities and decide on the political programs that best go with them. We cannot restore the colonial system as it was before Pearl Harbor, counting on a comfortable margin of time in which to decide how far we want to go toward emancipation, and how fast. Russia will not stand still. China will not wait long. The rest of the freedom bloc will press for change. If we stand still, the colonial peoples will begin to pull away from us and to gravitate toward the moving forces. In most parts of the world the idea of a cooling-off period is foolish. In Asia it is an invitation to disaster. We must have a policy now.

CHAPTER VIII

THE ESSENTIALS OF AN AMERICAN POLICY IN ASIA

BEFORE we can draw up an American policy we must decide what we intend to achieve by victory. It is better to have peace aims, and to state them. Even if we do not have them, or try to hide them, the things we do and do not do will soon reveal to the world the direction in which we are going, and whether we are going there on purpose or just drifting. It is better also to work for a stable peace than for a long armistice. Even if we fail to get a permanent peace we are likely, merely by working for it, to get a long peace. The would-be realists who think only of a long armistice and a good position in the next war would only lead us to a worse war than they want, sooner than they want it.

Victory has been brought within reach only by the fact that the United Nations exist. Victory can lead to peace only through continuing agreement between the United Nations. The power to lay the foundations of peace lies primarily with America, Britain, Russia, and China – not individually but collectively. If they cannot get along with each other, then sooner or later one or the other of them will begin to experiment individually with getting along with Germany or Japan, before we have decided collectively that it is proper to admit Germany and Japan to the future world organization — and the maneuvering for good positions in the next war will have begun. We must, in planning an American policy, give full weight to what our allies need as well as to what we want. We must act with our allies in giving the greatest possible scope, within the United Nations, to countries which have less military power than we do; and we must make the ranks of freedom easy to join, so that all countries and peoples may enter the United Nations and expand it into a world organization.

Victory in Asia will bring us the first problem of policy in imposing terms on Japan. We must do our thinking about this problem now. Our representatives, when discussing policy with the representatives of our allies, should not be weakened by a confused and divided public opinion; and if our representatives make concessions to what our allies want, the public, in turn, must know why the concessions are justifiable.

Japan, like Germany, must be deprived of the power of resorting to aggression. Fortunately, Japan does not have, in its home islands, the industrial raw materials which Germany has; Japanese industry is not as complete and well rounded as that of Germany, and Japanese technology is much less versatile. Under the Cairo Declaration, it has already been decided that China is to recover the Northeastern Provinces (Manchuria), together with Formosa (Taiwan) and the Pescadores. These losses will leave the Japanese nation of about 75,000,000 people in an island territory of approximately 150,000 square miles – not quite as large as California. Most of her fleet and merchant ships and a large part of her heavy industry will have been destroyed before the war ends.

In strictly military terms the problem of security is therefore relatively simple. Japan can be kept under observation from American island bases farther to the south, and from Russian and Chinese bases. The most important problem is to avoid competition in armaments among the United Nations, and for this reason it is important that any further territory taken from Japan, such as the Pacific islands, the Kuriles, or Southern Sakhalin, over and above the territories listed in the Cairo Declaration, should not be snatched by one of the victors but allotted by agreement of the United Nations. Air and sea patrol of Japan could be kept up for as long as necessary in one of two ways: either an international security force, of the kind discussed at Dumbarton Oaks, could be based on islands near Japan, or American, British, Russian, and Chinese forces could, by agreement, make use of each other's bases. An international security force would be preferable.

More important is the industrial disarmament of Japan and the prevention of a future secret war industry. The question of a "hard" or "soft" peace is directly related to this problem. There is great danger that the use of these terms will lead away from realities into emotional discussion. We must not let ourselves be distracted from the basic fact: defeat will in itself impose a hard peace on Japan. The industrial imperialists and military imperialists, working together, had built up a system combining control of raw materials outside Japan with control of selling markets. This system will automatically be destroyed when Japan surrenders her conquests. Of the 75,000,000 Japanese, 40 per cent will then be engaged in an agriculture which is not quite able to feed the country, while 60 per cent will be engaged in a damaged industry dependent for both supplies and markets on the consent of the United Nations.

We must avoid confusing industrial demilitarization with disindustrialization. In a Japan deprived of all industry, people would starve by the million. (In pre-industrial Japan, the population numbered at most about 30,000,000, and increase was kept down by famines and by the widespread practice of abortion and infanticide.) We have never hated an enemy as we hate the Japanese, but we do not hate them to the point of starving several million of them. Japan must be left with some industry. It would be wise to warn the Japanese industrialists that if the army resorts to scorched-earth tactics in destroying industrial installations in the Northeastern Provinces and Korea, the equipment will have to be replaced out of Japan's home stock. This threat would do more to divide the industrialists and militarists than ideological propaganda. Apart from war measures of this kind, the wise policy is to forbid the manufacture of automobile and airplane engines, dismantle armament factories and naval yards, and let the rest of Japan's industry survive if it is able to survive under conditions of the world market. Because of the scarcity of raw materials in Japan, the stockpiling of military industrial materials can be prevented by checking imports of raw materials against production and export figures.

With this policy there could be combined, for as long as necessary, a policy of channeling Japan's industrial output toward the rehabilitation and the supply of consumer goods in devastated areas. Reparations can be handled partly by this method. It is impossible to settle reparations by confiscation except for transferring to China and Korea all Japanese property in Chinese and Korean territory, and the devastated and plundered countries in Asia do not have the manpower shortage which might make them call for reparations in the form of conscripted Japanese labor. By planning and directing Japan's output, however, the Japanese can be kept alive and at the same time be made to serve the over-all economic needs of Asia. The degree to which they co-operate in doing this successfully can be made one of the standards for judging Japan's fitness, eventually, to be admitted to the future world organization.

The question of the ownership and management of Japan's industries leads into the problem of the political handling of Japan. The Zaibatsu, or giant combines controlled by a few families, are well known. These families have had immense power over the state, and have supplied a great part of the motor energy driving the military mechanism. The only way to break their power over the state is to give the state power over them. Their holdings, and the vast holdings of the Emperor and Imperial Household in banks, insurance, shipping, and other large corporations, as well as in industry, should be funded and placed under a Ministry of Economics and the Ministry of Finance, where they can be supervised as long as is necessary by a United Nations control commission.

The political effect of this would be to make possible the rise of a new generation of technicians, administrators, and executives loyal to the state. The rate at which such a class emerges and takes hold of things will help to determine the time at which economic autonomy should be returned to Japan. It will be necessary, of course, to exclude from such service the inside, trusted executives of the Zaibatsu, who encouraged a feudal type of devotion and loyalty among their picked employees. Among the lower-paid, professionally qualified men, however, there will be found ample numbers who will soon attach themselves loyally to the principle of promotion on merit in the public service.

New loyalties are formed only by men who get a new chance in life. They therefore require a change in system and a change in symbol. This is the key to the problem of the Japanese Emperor. At the present time there is a deceptive unanimity among American experts in agreeing that we should not make ourselves responsible, in the eyes of the Japanese people, either for deposing the Japanese Emperor or for maintaining him. This apparent unanimity actually covers a wide range of disagreement. There are those who think we should not intervene, because unless we intervene the Japanese people will themselves abolish the imperial institution. Others believe that if we do not intervene the imperial institution will remain and we shall either be able to use the present Emperor or to replace him with another whom we can make our mouthpiece to order the Japanese people to carry out whatever terms we impose.

As a matter of political prophecy, I agree that the Japanese people are likely to overturn the throne unless we prevent them. As a matter of political principle, I think we should make the worst possible mistake in trying to use for our own purposes either the present Emperor or a successor nominated by us. It has long been a convention in Japan that those who have power express their power by putting words in the mouth of the emperor. The militarists have identified themselves with this convention and it must therefore be destroyed. It can only be destroyed by showing that there are kinds of power which do not need to use an emperor. If we were to make use of the Emperor, then after our withdrawal the power to use him would not pass to representatives of a democratic government, but would revert to the militarists.

When Japan is defeated terrorists of the Black Dragon type, and many individual militarists, will go underground. If the Emperor continues in apparent power, and the voice of authority continues to be the imperial voice, they will be able to persuade people that the old system still exists and can be restored in full. On the other hand the underground terrorists and militarists will die off, failing to make recruits and perpetuate themselves, if we help to make possible new activities and new loyalties which are profitable to those who profess them, and at the same time make it possible for them to divert their thoughts in new directions. Belief in things like imperial divinity has no natural place in an age of chemistry, plastics, electronics, and stratosphere navigation; it can survive only with the aid of assiduous indoctrination, and if we lend support to that indoctrination while we are in

Japan, then after we leave it will be used not by those who are looking forward to the future but by those who are looking back to the past.[1]

If the Japanese themselves decide to do without an emperor, well and good. If not, we should show that militarism has been so catastrophically defeated that we, the victors, do not need to use the Emperor. He and all males eligible for the throne by Japanese rules of succession and adoption should be interned, preferably in China but under the supervision of a United Nations commission, to emphasize united responsibility. His estates, and estates belonging to members of Zaibatsu families and important militarists, should be made over to an agrarian reform program, conspicuously without his sanction and by order of the United Nations. Eventually, after his death and after a new civil service and a new management of finance and industry have taken hold, the remaining members of the imperial line can be allowed to go where they like. New vested interests will by that time be able to prevent the restoration of a monarchy.

I assume that the Japan of the future will be a republic. In helping the Japanese to launch this republic we should draw confidence from the fact that Japan has a larger literate electorate than any

[1] One of the few who have noted this point is T. A. Bisson, whose article on "The Price of Peace for Japan" in *Pacific Affairs*, March 1944, is among the best yet published.

other country in Asia. It failed to create strong democratic governments in the past not because it was politically stupid, but because it could not change the constitution and because militarist and terrorist organizations were unchecked. In spite of all repression, however, the Japanese elections of 1936 showed a heavy vote against military adventurism. In the first interim government we should include political and parliamentary leaders still surviving who have a record of imprisonment or of being beaten up by political gangsters, or threatened with assassination. To protect them from terror we should include among war criminals all officers and civilians with proved associations of the Black Dragon type, who should be punished according to their guilt, with deportation and internment as the minimum. It will not be difficult to apprehend these criminals. The "secret" societies were secret only in a manner of speaking. The more dangerous terrorists were well known and boasted of their associations.

We must, on the other hand, not be soft with the old-school-kimono "liberals," from Prince Konoye on down, who used to entertain the Embassy crowd so charmingly and made such a good impression on Wall Street, art collectors, and members of the Garden Club. They belong in Japan to the stratum which in Germany produced Schacht; they were part of the liaison between predatory militarism and predatory big business. When Japan begins to show an ability to make progress politically, we must expect the leadership to be left of center and at least liberal enough to be friendly with Russia. Friendly relations with Russia and China will in fact be as necessary for a democratic Japan as friendly relations with us.

We ourselves cannot keep in separate compartments our China policy, our Soviet policy, our Japan policy, or our policy toward colonial countries. Nowhere is this more evident than in China. The Chinese have a vast territory and the largest homogeneous population in the world. They are potentially one of the great powers, but economically they have been bled white and politically they have not yet evolved a representative government relying on votes instead of on the armed forces of political groups and provincial magnates. We need political stability and economic prosperity in China so that we can invest our capital there safely and sell our products in an expanding market. If we sell to China we can also buy from China, but it is not to our interest to buy from 450,000,000 people who sell cheaply because their labor is sweated. Whether they sell to us or to others, they pull down the world standard of living, and our long-term interest is in selling goods of high quality to prosperous customers all over the world.

We do not want China to become dependent on us. If we ever find the Chinese Government becoming dependent on us to the point where it cannot deal with other governments without our backing, or would be overthrown by its own people unless we supported it, it will mean that we have gone beyond the safe limits of a direct foreign policy and should refer all questions of policy, military, political, and economic, to the United Nations. Otherwise, there would be grave danger of conflict between our China policy and that of Russia or that of Great Britain.

Our relations with China today are getting uncomfortably close to this limit of safety. The immediate steps which must be taken are political, rather than economic or military. Our naval victories and our recovery of the Philippines are rapidly creating a situation which has far-reaching military connotations for China. At what point shall we reach the coast of China? What Chinese forces will be there to join up with us? What will their relation be to the Chinese Government and High Command? These questions cannot be answered without political decisions at the highest levels. There is a comparable situation in the north, where Russian entry into the war against Japan would bring into the open an imperative need for political and military co-ordination.

It is essential that America should cease to be so conspicuously the main link between China and the United Nations. Our interests are great, but they are not isolated. Our China policy must be brought into proper liaison with our Soviet and

British policies. There are political and economic decisions to be made without which military decisions cannot be properly exploited. They must not be made separately, but with due regard to the fact that they dovetail into each other. It is misleading to say that nothing can be done until Russia is at war against Japan. Earlier in the war Russia, in spite of the risk of offending Japan, supplied China with as much war material over the little-advertised Sinkiang Road as we did over the Burma Road. There was at that time a good general understanding between the Russians and the Chinese. The Russians made no deliveries to the Chinese Communists; on the contrary, they kept up their supplies to the National Government even though they knew some of the material was being allotted to armies blockading the Chinese Communists.

The Sinkiang Road, which could easily be made much more important, has actually become very much less important, because the general understanding between Russia and China is now bad. America, acting alone as middleman, cannot successfully bring the Chinese and the Russians together. There is too much danger of a drift toward making China a Poland in Asia, with America eventually identified as the not too enthusiastic backer of a "legitimist" group with too many Chinese "Polish colonels" and not enough popular support, and Russia identified as the strategically placed backer of a group which is legally "dissident," but has growing support among moderate groups as well as the peasants.

Britain and France must also be brought in. In the colonial world, China has a common frontier with Britain in Burma. The frontier lies largely in tribal country where the people are neither Chinese nor Burmese; it is not fully demarcated, and is open to a number of disputes involving mineral resources. China also has a common frontier with Indo-China, and is a close neighbor of Thailand, whose future as a free country will have an important effect on the shaping of colonial policy. On the southern coast of China, after the war, there will have to be clarification of the status and future of Hong Kong, which is a British possession, the adjoining territory of Kowloon, leased to the British, and the territory of Kwangchowwan, leased to France. These bits of territory cannot be compared in strategic importance with the immense Russo-Chinese land frontier; but they involve test questions which will determine over-all political attitudes.

It is of primary importance to the future organization of peace that in dealing with Britain and France China should be associated with Russia as well as America, and in dealing with Russia should be identified as a member of a group which includes Britain and France as well as America. Emphasis of this kind on the United Nations as a group would have a steadying effect not only on Asia but on Anglo-French-Russian relations in Europe.

Most important of all, only emphasis on the United Nations as a group can provide a strong framework for the future of the Northeastern Provinces. If China's allies as a group have a common policy directed toward the political and economic integration of China, the future of the Northeastern Provinces – the most important base for the future heavy industry of China – will be assured. If China disintegrates, the breakup will be territorial as well as political. The British on the Burma frontier and in South China, as well as the Russians in the Northeastern Provinces, will be forced to deal with local political entities. In dealing with an increasingly unified, centralized China, the Russians can easily negotiate what economic facilities they need in transit across the Northeastern Provinces and shipment from Dairen, without demanding occupation or control of railways or harbors. If the tendency of China is to fall apart, the British in the strategic southwestern area and at Hong Kong on the coast, and the Russians in the Northeastern Provinces and at Dairen and Port Arthur, will feel a strong pressure to take steps to ensure minimum local control.

Obviously, the primary responsibilities and decisions lie with the Chinese themselves. Their country and their society are theirs to build. The responsibility of China's allies is to show that their support for constructive tendencies is collective and in the world interest, and not a race for individual advantage. Britain and America can successfully support their legitimate capitalist interests in China, and at the same time work in co-operation with the Russians for democratic harmony in a country in which the second largest party is Communist. The Russians have already shown that their interest in China is not limited to the Communists, by supplying munitions to China as a country and not to the Communists as a faction, thus establishing the evidence that there are terms on which they are ready to co-operate. We on our part must learn to associate our problems and opportunities in China and in other countries and avoid isolating them. China is but a major example of the new world situation. The world is now grouped in three major divisions. In one, the capitalist economic system and democratic political system are vigorous and unshaken. In another the Communist (or strictly speaking, the socialist) political system is now permanently established and identified with a collectivist economic system. In the third, there is an adjustment yet to be made between capitalism and collectivism, and mixed political orders have not yet clearly taken shape. There will be a number of them, showing many degrees of modification, and the greatest of all the problems of our time is to work out methods of adjustment and avoid irreconcilable divisions both within countries and between countries.

In China we should take the following steps: –

1. We should emphasize consultation between the American, British, and Soviet Ambassadors and their military and economic attachés.

2. We should urge a four-power conference to co-ordinate economic and military supplies over the Burma Hump, the Sinkiang Road, and, as soon as possible, ports on the coast. (We must not assume that economic problems will be solved as soon as our ships can reach the coast. China's internal transportation system is weak, and the other routes will remain important for the hinterland.)

3. The United Nations collectively should encourage the Chinese Government to grant immediately a substantial part of the program of election, referendum, and recall projected by Sun Yat-sen himself. Though this is the official program of the Kuomintang, it has never been implemented.

4. As soon as democratic processes have indisputably begun to work, we should advocate (and if asked to, assist in carrying out) a reorganization of the National Army and the disbandment of superfluous troops. We should avoid isolating the problem of the Communist troops, remembering that there are also not only war-lord troops, but regular troops which, while nominally part of the National Army, are in fact Kuomintang Party troops. The military corollary of a democratic system is an army which is not under the control or indoctrination of one party alone.

5. Through the Treasury and the Foreign Eco-

nomic Administration we should do our utmost to revive production in China, emphasizing the value of the profit motive, and therefore of private enterprise, in getting production going quickly.[2] We should of course avoid encroaching on the right of the Chinese Government to use its credit, and its power to create capital through taxation, to finance such state enterprises as it sees fit. We should work closely with the Chinese Ministries of Finance and Economics, and also consult frequently with Britain and Russia. We should try to make an early application in China of the principles of United Nations financial and economic co-operation drafted at the Bretton Woods Conference, which are the economic parallel to the Dumbarton Oaks draft for political co-operation.

Now, during the war, is the time to gain an insight into China's postwar economic needs. Our capital surplus is great, but not unlimited. After the war there will be demands for it from other countries besides China. We should place our money and our exports with a view to more than quick profits; we need to foster long-term economic trends favorable to our ways of producing goods and doing business. The Bretton Woods proposals assume a large volume of private investment and also a need for co-ordinating monetary and economic policies

[2] Mr. Donald Nelson's mission to help set up a Chinese War Production Board is an excellent example of the right kind of measure.

between governments. We should favor the setting up of the machinery proposed at Bretton Woods, and should use it in China and elsewhere in Asia to combine the maximum volume of private investment with the greatest possible harmony between the economic policies of the Chinese Government and our government and the governments of other countries which have capital and capital goods to export.

Co-operation with Russia in strengthening China will make it easier to co-operate with Russia in many other ways. We must begin, however, by recognizing—and remedying—the fact that the difficulty in dealing with Russia is not Russian policy, but the truly appalling lack of an American policy. The average American is as weak in this respect as the State Department. The usual discussion of Russia begins and ends with speculation about what Russia is going to do. By this kind of speculation we reveal that we still completely misread the position of Russia. The question is not what Russia is going to do, but what we are going to do. Russia will act only when we have sufficiently revealed the direction in which we are going, and she will be able to act with equal decisiveness whether we show that we are moving by choice or merely by drift.

In Asia, even more than in Europe, the Russians hold a position in which they can outwait anybody. It is up to us to declare the rules of the game. Militarily, politically, and economically, if we declare for co-operation they are in a position to co-operate and to make it work. If we declare for a policy of independent grabbing of strategic bases, economic spheres of influence, and political satellites, they can outgrab us right down the line. It is we who create the circumstances for Russian action. The most dangerous blind spot in our whole concept of international relations is the fact that we do not realize that by doing nothing whatever we still create the circumstances for action by others.

Russia holds the key position at the top of the Pacific, looking down on Japan and touching both China's Northeastern Provinces and Korea. Either by agreement or, if we do not make that possible, by unilateral action, Russia will develop the strongest land-based air power in the North Pacific and a navy and a merchant marine in the Pacific. We cannot isolate or encircle Russia. The Soviet-Chinese land frontier is as immune to interference from us as the Canadian-American frontier is immune to Russian interference. Russia's political leverage in Korea, and in the long run in Japan, can be made much greater than ours. It is time for us to stop speculating and make a bid.

The essential bid is to invite co-operation in making a workable reality out of the Dumbarton Oaks draft for a United Nations world organization and the Bretton Woods draft for an International Monetary Fund and an International Bank for Reconstruction and Development.

Remembering that Soviet Asia has a common frontier with Afghanistan, and therefore a channel to India, we must in postwar United Nations policy planning bring the Russians all the way down to colonial Asia. Remembering the strong colonial feeling after the last war that the Russians were sympathetic people, we must assume that there will be an even stronger feeling of the same kind after this war. We must therefore seize the advantages of discussing all major world policy in common council with the Russians, and avoid isolating Russia, because it would actually isolate us more than the Russians. As compensation – and remembering that before Pearl Harbor the British capital invested in China was much greater than ours, and British enterprises more varied and widely spread – we must bring the British all the way up to Japan and Korea, in equal council.

In recent months there have been reports, of varying authenticity but collectively significant, that Russia wants a voice in the control of the Kiel Canal, a share in the Suez Canal, and a share in the development of oil resources in Iran. These reports could easily be taken as an indication of Russia's aggressive intention to "interfere" in all directions around her frontiers. I think, however, that they are more likely to mean that Russia is ready to abandon the old economic isolation and self-sufficiency which was the natural complement of the political isolation forced on her by the capitalist world. The reports may indicate that Russia is aware of a need for interests and activities, as well as policies, in the areas in which the influences of the capitalist-democratic world will meet those of the collectivist-socialist world. Certainly it can be argued that the discussion of purely theoretical agreement in policy tends to endless discussion and cautious reservations, while agreement on interlocking interests can be reached quickly by the executive decision of realists. We should, therefore, in an area like Korea, standing on Russia's frontier, invite Russia as soon as the war situation permits to join America, Britain, and China not only in political responsibility but in economic activity.

In our attitude toward the colonial possessions of Britain, Holland, and France we must modify our stand in principle for rapid emancipation. It is not up to us to force our allies to liberate their colonial subjects. On the other hand we should keep it on the record, by repeated official statements on official occasions, that any American forces engaged in joint operations in colonial territory are there only to drive out the Japanese, not to help our allies to restore colonial rule. As soon as the intensity of the war against Japan permits, we should withdraw our forces from such territories. We must not allow the idea to be spread, even by implication, that colonial reconquest is an American war aim; it is not in fact a war aim, but a consequence of victory over Japan.

Beyond this point we must feel our way. Current ideas about colonial policy range from complete restoration of the powers and responsibilities of the ruling countries (advocated by groups which have a vested interest in the colonial system) to the setting up of an international trustee authority. A halfway proposal is to require the ruling country to report periodically to an international authority on its colonial stewardship.

We should start at this halfway point and carry it a little farther than halfway when the time comes to elaborate the Dumbarton Oaks draft charter proposals. Colonial questions embrace questions of economic and political interest, which could be brought under the jurisdiction of the Economic and Social Council which is in the Dumbarton Oaks draft, or under a specially created Council for Dependent Peoples. The question of security is also involved. The value of independence depends partly on how safe the world is made for new nations, especially those that are small and weak. The security aspect could be dealt with by the Security Council. On this Council Britain, and France in due course, would be permanent members with veto votes and could defend their own interests and those of Holland.

There are a number of colonial issues and problems for which access to world public opinion needs to be provided. There is, for instance, the question of minorities within colonial peoples. In the present deadlock in India, the British authorities take the position that the Moslems and Hindus must first come to terms with each other; only then can the British discuss with them the details of independence. This ruling sounds impartial in principle, but does not work out fairly in practice. It enables the minority to put undue pressure on the majority by threatening not to come to terms at all, and thus to defer independence indefinitely.

Another problem is the deciding of the relative level of political maturity at which a subject people can properly be given independence. The Netherlands Indies, for instance, stretch from east to west for a distance greater than the width of North America, and contain a number of different peoples. Should the more sophisticated people of Java be given their independence earlier than the less sophisticated peoples of Dutch Borneo and Dutch New Guinea, or should the whole political entity be kept intact, as in the Philippines, where there are also minority groups and backward peoples? The best solution is to set a date, or a series of dates, and to make it the responsibility of the ruling power to prepare each people for political independence by the agreed date. Owing to peculiar circumstances the Americans were willing to set a date in the Philippines and thus to establish as a practical precedent what would otherwise have been regarded as a romantic notion; but we must recognize that in other cases it will not be so easy for the ruling power, as an interested party, to set a date which satisfies the subject people. Here again a Council for Dependent Peoples could ease the pressure between rulers and subject peoples.

Finally, we must deal with the fact that colonies represent the division of the sources of raw materials. The economic practices of colonial powers vary a good deal, but the general tendency is for vested interests whose policy is to safeguard cheap raw-material supplies to block interests which would otherwise be active in raising colonial standards of living in order to expand their selling markets. The only satisfactory approach to this problem is through a general policy of expanding investments and markets, which could be set in motion through the International Monetary Fund and International Bank for Reconstruction and Development, as proposed at the Bretton Woods Conference. A successful international program of economic expansion would eliminate many narrow national interests, and by raising standards of living would also contribute to education and to political maturity.

Subsidiary to planned economic improvement there should be a plan for financing colonial administrative expenses out of increased profits, credited to an international colonial fund. Normally, the salaries and pensions of colonial administrators are paid out of local taxes, which means that senior civil servants, as the time draws near for their retirement, become unduly conservative. Fearing that independence of the people they have been ruling will lead to repudiation of their pensions, they tend unconsciously to see the reasons for deferring independence more clearly than the reasons for hastening it. An international funding of this responsibility would straighten out a key administrative problem.

Most colonial administrators are professionally sensitive to the dangers of going too fast. These dangers exist; but they are not so great, under present conditions, as the dangers of going too slowly. Compromises and interim programs will be necessary in many colonial questions, but at every stage we should make it the American principle to go ahead, taking reasonable risks, and to distrust the supposed safety of not going ahead.

The war will end with the greatest aggregate of the world's industrial productive plant and military, naval, and air power in the hands of the capitalist nations. Second in power of all kinds will be the collectivist system of the Soviet Union. In addition to these two there will be the colonial countries and the relatively undeveloped nations. Formerly, these were regarded as a margin of expansion for the great capitalist countries. In the future, they can no longer be so treated. To a certain extent, they will remain marginal to the capitalist countries, but to a certain extent they will also become marginal to collectivist Russia. Some of the countries which once imported capital controlled by corporations set up as private corporations (even if, like a number of oil companies, they were state-aided or state-owned) will in the future import some of their capital from Russia.

There will also be countries, once colonial or politically subordinate, which after the war will be free. For the most part, these newly free countries will be included in the capitalist part of the world; but some of them will be strongly influenced by contact with the collectivist part.

In all of these new and changing relationships, Asia will be of critical importance. Asia will largely determine the degree to which the capitalist world and the collectivist world can co-operate. The value and significance of freedom for the newly free peoples will also be put to the proof first and foremost in Asia. No longer, therefore, can we think of Asia simply as an area of overflow for our surplus energies. Asia will become, instead, a testing ground for all our theories and ways of doing things. Failure in Asia would doom our hopes for a co-operative world order. Success in Asia would prove the survival value of the postwar world order toward which we are working. The time has come to give Asiatic policy a top priority in America's relations with the world.

INDEX

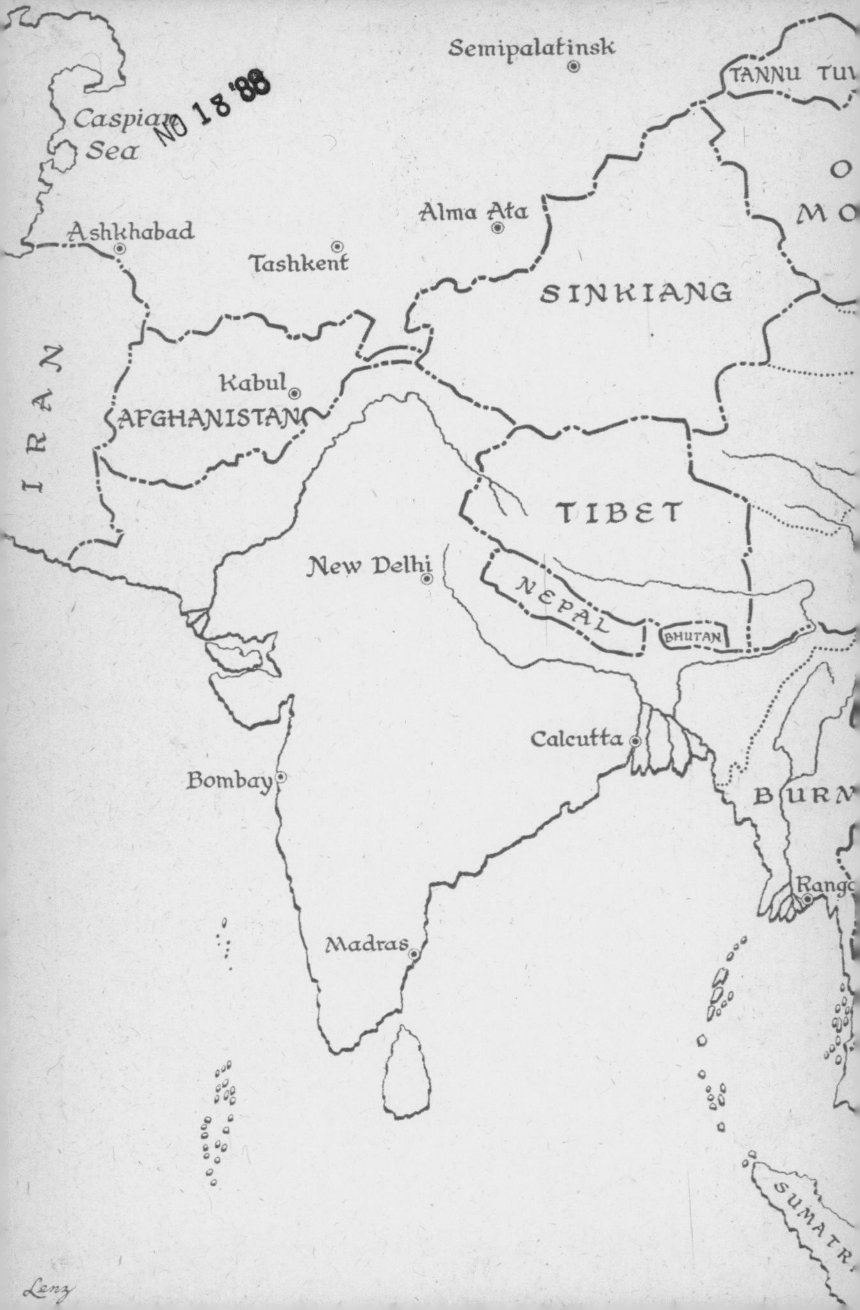
Semipalatinsk
TANNU TU
Caspian Sea
Alma Ata
Ashkhabad
Tashkent
SINKIANG
IRAN
Kabul
AFGHANISTAN
TIBET
New Delhi
NEPAL
BHUTAN
Calcutta
Bombay
BURM
Rang
Madras
SUMATR
Lenz